...turned unto fables...

...they will not endure sound doctrine...

REV. R. CARLTON BALLOWE

iUniverse, Inc.
Bloomington

...turned unto fables...
...they will not endure sound doctrine...

iUniverse books may be ordered through booksellers or by contacting:

iUniverse
1663 Liberty Drive
Bloomington, IN 47403
www.iuniverse.com
1-800-Authors (1-800-288-4677)

*Because of the dynamic nature of the Internet, any web addresses or links contained in this
book may have changed since publication and may no longer be valid. The views expressed
in this work are solely those of the author and do not necessarily reflect the views of the
publisher, and the publisher hereby disclaims any responsibility for them.*

*Any people depicted in stock imagery provided by Thinkstock are models,
and such images are being used for illustrative purposes only.*

Certain stock imagery © Thinkstock.

ISBN: 978-1-4759-4100-5 (sc)
ISBN: 978-1-4759-4101-2 (hc)
ISBN: 978-1-4759-4102-9 (e)

Printed in the United States of America

iUniverse rev. date: 8/13/2012

Contents

Introduction

SOME ARE GIVEN A burden for the lost that are outside the will of God. Others are grieved more by those within the church that do not know the unspeakable joy of the abundant life. As much as it pains me to see both these groups fail to realize all that God has for them, my real burden is for the church as a whole and the doctrinal purity upon which it will stand or fall. Please understand that doctrinal purity in this context has nothing to do with adhering to a set of beliefs passed down by any person or group of people. Pure doctrine is based on truth derived from the source, unfiltered by people or groups with ulterior motives.

The Bible tells us the end of the earth will be preceded by a time of Great Tribulation; the natural consequence of a depraved mankind being led by masters of deceit. In this caldron of chaos, confusion, and deception, people will be desperate for an anchor of truth, strength, and stability. If the church is to be that anchor, people will need to see that events are unfolding in a manner that verifies the truth of what the church has been teaching. Only then, will the church have the credibility it must have if it is to play a positive role in the lives of as many people as possible. Unfolding events will soon expose anything less than pure doctrinal truth as error. If the church is still clinging to and promoting errors when they begin to be exposed; people will turn away from the church as a potential source of truth. This is already happening. If we don't take immediate steps to purify our doctrine by ridding it of the "itching ears theology" that has crept in, we will undermine our mission to reach the lost, both now and in the future.

As an institution, the church has lost its passion for truth and is no longer preparing the saints to recognize and deal with the false prophets and false doctrines that have, as predicted, become so pervasive (Mt. 24-11 & 24). Likewise, the church is not preparing the saints to withstand the persecution and tribulation that is part of the run-up to the date the world has with Armageddon (Rev. 13:7). Indeed, churches have become part of the problem. Most promote a form of "itching ears theology" that is based more on filling the pews and coffers than on sound doctrine. To compete for "contributors", they have stretched the positive while glossing over and watering down the hard truths. This has gone on to the point that much of what emanates from pulpits today is bordering on fairy tale and many believers have been "turned unto fables" (2nd Tim 4:4).

In an effort to appeal to the world, the church is losing its soul. It's a very short, steep, and slippery slope between putting a positive spin on an ugly truth and perverting the gospel. When the church began to put a positive "spin" on doctrine in order to win converts (aka contributors), those doctrines were bound to devolve into the "*doctrines of devils*". We would do well to heed Jesus' warning from Matthew 16:6, "*Take heed and beware of the leaven of the Pharisees and of the Sadducees*". We know from verse 12 that He wasn't talking about bread; *Then understood they how that he bade them not beware of the leaven of bread, but of the doctrine of the Pharisees and of the Sadducees.* What an apt analogy; doctrinal error is just like leaven; once it is introduced, it spreads almost supernaturally throughout the loaf. Such are the fables that pass for doctrine today. Apart from a remnant that God is never without, the whole church is infected.

How did this leaven get into the loaf? From the very beginning the church began to split into factions and compete for followers.

Differing doctrinal positions were behind most of the splits. We see the earliest examples in Acts Chapter 15 involving some of the heroes of our faith. Paul and Barnabas were said to be involved in *"no small dissension and disputation"* with people promoting doctrine with which Paul and Barnabas disagreed (15:2). Even when the matter was taken to the highest levels, there was still *"much disputing"* (15:7). Ultimately, Peter's well thought out argument won the day and at least the apostles weren't split. The point is that doctrinal issues have been, and always will be, with us. As long as they are decided on the basis of fidelity to truth, there is no problem. When the question of appeal becomes a factor in determining doctrinal positions, we don't just invite error, we invite evil. It's all the opening the Devil needs to introduce and eventually substitute his watered down and powerless perversion of the gospel.

Unfortunately, appeal was allowed to become a factor. Indeed, I believe it has become a major factor in the modern era. The sects, that we now call denominations, may have been born out of pure doctrinal differences; but ultimately, in order to survive, they had to frame those differences in ways that appeal to prospective followers; even if that meant rounding off the rough edges of truth. These new doctrines were then taught by the colleges and seminaries established by the denominations for the purpose of indoctrinating new pastors. Pastors are almost compelled to accept the doctrine of the denomination in charge of the school, college, or seminary they attend; and members of the pastor's church are pretty well trained not to question the pastor's doctrine as long as it is in line with the denomination.

Consequently, error, introduced for the sake of appeal, is nearly impossible to purge from the system. Any attempt at correction has three strikes against it before it even starts. The indoctrination process insures the error will be taught to all incoming pastors. The appeal that led the church to adopt the error in the first place is not likely to be overcome by congregants who are largely apathetic when it comes to issues of doctrine. Finally, not many people have a "burden" for the church as a whole and even fewer see doctrinal purity as the basis upon which the church will either rise or fall. Accepting second, third, or fourth hand doctrine based on another person's understanding of truth is a lot less time consuming. You can quote a lot of statistics from a lot of different sources to show that even born again Christians don't read their Bibles. Only about 35% of Christians even claim to read them on a regular basis. A much smaller percentage; about 5%, have ever read the Bible cover to cover. Since these people spend little time in the Word of truth, they have no basis for questioning second hand doctrine, or developing their own. It pains me to say it, but based on these figures, and other evidence, there aren't a lot of lovers of truth even among those who claim to serve the God of truth. Where are the Bereans of our day?

In Acts Chapter 17 and verse 11, Luke says of the people of Berea; *"11These were more noble than those in Thessalonica, in that they received the word with all readiness of mind, and searched the scriptures daily, whether those things were so."* From seminary lecterns, to pulpits, to pews, Bereans are an endangered species. Professors teach what the denomination has adopted. Pastors accept what they are being taught in seminary. And the faithful accept what they are being taught from the pulpit. They may go so far as to memorize key components of the messages they hear, and if called upon, they may be able to regurgitate the salient points, but no one is following the path of the Bereans and searching the scriptures daily to see if what they are being taught is truth. Real learning takes place when we mine for additional sources of evidence to either corroborate or refute what we are being taught. Although the Bible tells us this is a "noble" endeavor, it simply does not appear to be happening.

In fairness to those individuals who did not embarked on a quest for truth in the past, I would acknowledge that not too long ago, questioning church orthodoxy in pursuit of truth was considered heresy and was punishable by death. I would also acknowledge that until the relatively recent past, most lay people were illiterate. They had little choice but to accept the doctrines they were taught. Many charlatans and hucksters throughout ancient and modern history have used this fact to con the faithful. But this is the information age. Almost all of us are literate. We have Bibles and electronic Bibles with built in concordances and commentaries. We can do word studies, topic studies, people studies, event studies, etc. A world of information is literally at our fingertips. Access to knowledge has exploded (Dan 12:4). We are without excuse. With a little effort and the right spirit, we can find doctrinal truth. If we claim to love the God of truth while remaining dispassionate about the pursuit of truth, we contradict ourselves.

The question is....how many of us are really lovers and seekers of truth? Everything about the last days and the people of power and influence will be based on deception. The Bible tells us, all but the very elect will be taken in by the distortions and those who *"received not the love of the truth"* will perish (Mt 24:24 & 2ⁿᵈ Thes 2:10). Now, more than ever, the ability to distinguish between truth and a sales pitch, propaganda, or spin, is quite literally, becoming a matter of eternal life and death.

The purpose of this book is to ignite a love of truth and critical thinking in the heart of everyone who reads it. I want to create a whole new class of "Bereans" who can use the sword of the Word to rightly divide truth from error. Perhaps then, we can begin to purge the church of "itching ears theology". To the extent that we fail, the church will still be promoting these "fables" when the real events of Revelation expose them for the errors they are. At that point, whatever small measure of credibility the church has remaining will be lost, and so will untold millions of souls that we might have reached if we had kept our credibility intact. There is so much riding on the credibility of the church, we must try to reclaim it to the fullest extent possible.

Chapter One

. . . turned unto fables . . .

A LITTLE OVER A hundred years ago the Industrial Revolution began when a few enterprising individuals set out to mass produce items that had previously been fabricated to order by individual craftsmen such as blacksmiths, cobblers, carpenters, silversmiths, and etc.. For the first time, large numbers of workers were brought together under one roof. This concentration of labor naturally led to a concentration of housing as more and more people migrated to the urban areas to be near the factories that employed them. While the masses assembled in the urban areas for better access to the factories; an unintended consequence was better access to the masses. Instead of itinerant preachers having to travel by horseback to remote hills and hollows to reach small enclaves of individuals and families, they could set up tents near the urban centers and reach more people in a five night revival than in years of scouring sparsely populated areas. Thus the first incarnation of mass evangelism, the tent revival, was born of urbanization and the industrial revolution. This was quickly followed by the inventions of radio and television and a whole new level of mass evangelism was possible.

It is not surprising that when evangelicals set out to take advantage of this unprecedented access to the masses they began to apply product development, marketing, and distribution techniques borrowed from industry. In industry, "product development" means incorporating the most desirable features of various individual designs into a single hybrid that best combines mass appeal with simplicity of design. The single, simple, design facilitates mass production. The economies of scale inherent in mass production lower the cost and further enhance the products appeal. Marketing, of course, involves emphasizing all that is positive about a product while ignoring or downplaying the negative. Throw a little competition into the mix and the analogy to industry is complete. Now let's see if the analogy to industry will stand up under scrutiny.

"Mega ministries" were born when charismatic personalities gained unprecedented access to the masses. Perhaps they all began with pure motives; but in the end, the only certainty is that the survival of mega ministries is dependent on mega bucks, and mega bucks aren't generated without mega audiences. As the number of "evangelist" steadily increased, the competition for "supporters" became just as intense as the competition for customers in the corporate world. The key to surviving intense competition in the corporate world is developing and building a more appealing product. Ministries are not exempt from the laws of supply and demand that drive the rest of the world. Like corporations, their survival is dependent on developing and marketing a product that is more appealing than the one offered by the competition. This scramble for supporters / customers by competing ministries led to the adoption of doctrines with the broadest possible appeal across the widest possible spectrum of the population. These individual doctrines were then woven together to create a tapestry of "itching ears theology" that is prevalent in so many denominations and used by so many televangelist today. Marketing 101: emphasize the positive while diminishing the negative, and don't hesitate to test the limits of believability in doing so.

There is nothing inherently wrong with using the latest methodology in spreading the gospel, as long as the theology isn't compromised.

The earthly ministry of Christ reveals an unwavering theology of *whosoever believeth* (Jn 3:16) and a methodology of spreading it that varied considerably, even over a short period of time (Lk 10:4 & Lk 22:36). Paul was so flexible in his methodology that he felt we should be *all things to all men that* we *might by all means save some* (1st Cor 9:22). Like Christ and the apostles, we should vary our methods to gain a wider audience; but, if the message itself is watered down, the hearing will be inconsequential, or worse. I believe the line was crossed and theology has been compromised in the competition for "supporters".

So what happened when the gospel got the corporate treatment? In the initial product development stage it was reduced to a core message that was simple, uniform, and appealing; with the primary emphasis on appealing. After all, if your product has no appeal, it won't matter how efficiently you produce it, how well you market it, or what kind of distribution network you have.

With survival dependent on appeal, the decision to round the sharp edges off the "hard truths" was as difficult to resist as it was easy to rationalize. After all, they presumably wouldn't be in the ministry if they didn't think they were doing the Lord's work. Convinced of this, they would naturally view the lack of appeal as resistance from the Devil and just another obstacle to overcome. With this mindset, broadening the appeal of the gospel becomes part of carrying out the great commission.

This is where the corporate marketing strategy became incompatible with the gospel. The gospel is not a widget. It cannot be improved. Its appeal cannot be broadened. Its value is not in appeal, but rather, in its ability to transform the lives of those who get past its inherent lack of appeal. There is no appeal in coming to see ourselves as reprobates incapable of saving ourselves. A Galilean carpenter that was crucified among common thieves doesn't readily appeal to the senses as a natural choice for a savior. The idea that we must willfully become a servant, surrendering our will and our lives, certainly doesn't sound very appealing. In a very fundamental way, the main aspects of the gospel are well beyond unappealing; they are downright offensive; intentionally so. Both Paul and Peter refer to the gospel as a "rock of offence" (Ro 9:33 & 1st Ptr 2:8). In Galatians 5:11, Paul talks about the "offence of the cross".

It is not appeal that brings us to salvation. Those who approach the throne because they perceive that there is something in it for them (a better life; eternal security; etc.) are on the wrong track. We don't find salvation in the quest for self-interest. Consider Psalm 34:18; *The LORD is nigh unto them that are of a broken heart; and saveth such as be of a contrite spirit.* This verse is one of many that sound the same theme. God doesn't want your burnt offerings and He sure doesn't want you approaching from the standpoint of what benefits you can get from it. *The sacrifices of God are a broken spirit: a broken and a contrite heart, O God, thou wilt not despise.* (Ps 51:17)

Unfortunately, mass marketing techniques have been applied to the gospel message and many doctrines have been selected and adapted with an eye toward broadening their appeal (we'll get into this more in later chapters). In many cases the appealing spin they put on the message may have brought people into the church. Some of these people may have recited the sinner's prayer and made a public profession of faith. All of this is to no avail if they were motivated by self-interest and unwilling to humbly surrender because their hearts and spirits were not sufficiently broken. They may have succeeded in getting people into the pews and adding to the collection plate, which are the main objectives of far too many ministries today; but they also rounded the sharp offensive edges off the hard truths until what they were left with was devoid of the power to save.

Sharp offensive edges are part of the camouflage God used to hide his plan from the wise and prudent while revealing it unto babes (Mt 11:25). It's one of the reasons no one ever rationalized their way to salvation. Round off the offensive edges and the result is a distortion that is devoid of power. Nevertheless, in a misguided effort at marketing, I'm afraid appeal became the driving force behind the formulation of doctrine.

The current generation is by no means the first to pervert doctrine in pursuit of cash. Johann (John) Tetzel, as far back as the early 1500s, was selling indulgences to raise money. His famously attributed slogan "As soon as the coin in the coffer rings, the soul from purgatory springs" was such a perversion of doctrine that it inspired Martin Luther to launch the Protestant Reformation. Although Tetzel's perversion of doctrine was limited in its reach by the absence of modern media, it nevertheless raised a lot of money.

The hucksters and charlatans who took to the airways with the advent of modern media have no such handicap. They shamelessly promote their prosperity theology in pursuit of dollars on a scale never before possible. The pitch may vary slightly, but the underlying theme is always, "The Lord wants all His faithful to be healthy, wealthy, prosperous, and wise. If you're not there yet, you just haven't been faithful enough; and you can correct that deficiency by faithfully supporting our ministry". What a scam! They are pure con artist. A large number of books have been written in recent years about televangelism and modern culture. If you wish to know more about how these con artists run their game, pick a few key words and do a google search. The purpose of this book is not to examine the mechanics of how they run their con, but rather, to look at the impact they have had on the doctrine promoted by the broader church and how this watered down doctrine is setting the church up for the "falling away" predicted in 2nd Thessalonians 2:3.

My basic premise is that the overwhelming majority of ministers started out with the conviction that they were on a mission to advance the kingdom. Unfortunately, having left seminary armed only with a glorified version of appealing half-truths, they were ill equipped to do so. When the sincere minister comes up against the shameless charlatan promoting an "itching ears" "prosperity theology", he will find his arsenal of half-truths inadequate, because they vary only in subtle detail from the message of the charlatan. In fact the differences are so subtle he may have a hard time convincing himself, let alone his flock, that the difference is worth the spiritual warfare. Most end up finding ways to slant the thrust of their own ministry toward ideas with the broadest possible appeal. While they would be repulsed by the notion of overtly lying, they routinely create false impressions by over emphasizing the simple and positive, while omitting the difficult and negative. They are being sucked into the vortex; the downward spiral that starts with shaving the rough edges off the truth, and ends with wholesale deception.

We live in a time when deception has been elevated to an art form. Politicians hire people called press secretaries whose sole purpose is to distort facts in such a way that the politician will be viewed more favorably than warranted. In point of fact "press secretary" itself is a deception. Press secretary is really a euphemism for "spin doctor", which is a euphemism for liar. Face it; any endeavor, the purpose of which is to place a degree of separation between an individual and the whole unvarnished truth, is a lie. We should not allow it to escape the label just because it is clever or subtle. But we have. As a society we have allowed, even embraced, the use of clever words and euphemisms to round the sharp edges off hard truths. This has been carried to the point that we even deny the hard truth that there are liars among us. In fact, using the word liar to describe someone who distorts truth has become more scandalous than being one!

During the Monica Lewinski affair, no one would use the word "lie". Those who had intentionally and knowingly denied the affair were not liars, they were prevaricators or obfuscators. They made "statements that were at variance with the facts". They "took liberties with the truth". They debated the meaning of "is". But no one used the word lie. One had to keep a dictionary handy, because the President's defenders trotted out every synonym or euphemism in the English language to keep from revealing the unvarnished truth that our president was a liar. To this day, even though he had to turn in his law license for lying under oath, no one in "polite" society will refer to his prevarications as lies or to him as a liar.

Euphemisms are rampant in our society. Many of them can seem relatively harmless, even humorous. A lot of people in my area are spreading "bio-solids" on their farm land. Even at this there has been considerable outcry. I can only imagine if they called it by some of its less euphemistic names, like sewage, human excrement, feces, or its four letter equivalent. We can make fun of euphemisms, but we shouldn't underestimate their power. "Friendly fire" sounds a lot better than being killed by your own people. "Assistance for the poor" has almost three times as much support as "welfare". The point is that speaking of things euphemistically can change how we feel about them. Tell people some government benefit is free and it will have almost universal support. Tell them the truth; that it is taxpayer funded, and it loses most of its appeal. My contention is that this pattern of rounding the edges off truth is always harmful. When the pattern finds its way into the church, it is potentially catastrophic. The whole of scripture depicts the struggle between truth and deception. Any compromise of the former brings us closer to the later. The Bible is very clear that deception, especially very subtle forms, will be the chief weapon of the Antichrist in the last days. Even a cursory reading of Matthew 24 and Revelation 13 will confirm this.

Truth is sometimes complicated and often very unpleasant. Falsehoods are often simple, and alluring. The only thing that stands between us and the gradual descent into an itching ears theology that will set the stage for the Antichrist is an unwavering commitment to unvarnished truth. Remember, Satan is the father of deception and subtlety is how he gets his foot in the door (Gen 3:1). The most dangerous error is the one that is closest to truth.

Without an almost fanatical commitment to absolute truth, even a person that means well can create a false impression from truth. Given this, imagine the error one bent on deception might be able to foist upon us. Consider the absolute truth that God is sovereign, loving, and gracious. If one oversimplifies this truth and emphasizes only the positive implications, the impression is created that if we accept Christ, He'll always provide for our every need and keep us safe. Ministries that depend on attracting and holding mega audiences focus almost exclusively on this half of the truth. But a half truth is a lie. This is especially so in matters of theology or doctrine.

While God is sovereign, loving, and gracious, the implications are not that simple. Bad things do happen to good people. With the exception of Jews, Christians are the most persecuted people in history. Countless millions have been starved, crucified, boiled in oil, skinned alive, sawed in two, fed to lions, and burned at the stake. The most righteous man born of woman lived in poverty and had his head served up on a platter (Mt 11:11 & 14:11). Consider the plight of the writer of half of the New Testament, the Apostle Paul. Speaking of himself in 2nd Corinthians 11:24-25 Paul said; "*Of the Jews five times received I forty stripes save one. Thrice was I beaten with rods, once was I stoned, thrice I suffered shipwreck, a night and a day I have been in the deep…*" Apparently he didn't consider being snake bitten, imprisoned, and threatened even worthy of mention. The exact circumstances of his death appear to be lost to history but it's a pretty safe bet he was eventually imprisoned and executed by the Romans. Tradition has it that he was beheaded. Glossing over, downplaying, or ignoring the fact that *we must through much tribulation enter into the kingdom of God* (Acts 14:22) turns sound doctrine into *itching ears* theology and truth into a *fable* (2 Tim 4:3-4). Itching ears theology is weakening the church and setting it up for the predicted "falling away".

Again, I want to stress that few ministers began with sinister motives. Many passages of scripture lend themselves to more than one interpretation. This is quite apparent from the number of denominations within the Christian community. Ambiguous passages of scripture must be interpreted by considering the overall context and making a decision based on a preponderance of all the Biblical evidence. But, no amount of energy or scholarship can remove all uncertainty from every text. There will always be different logical interpretations of difficult passages. Some interpretations will always be more appealing than others. Human nature will always predispose us toward adopting the more appealing interpretation. The problem doesn't arise so much from a specific or isolated instance of selecting a doctrinal position on the basis of appeal. The problem occurs when selection on the basis of appeal becomes systemic.

When a whole series of possible interpretations are selected on the basis of appeal and then woven together, the result won't be sound systematic theology or doctrine; it will be a fairy tale. I believe that modern competitive pressures and human predispositions have turned us away from sound doctrine and toward fables. The industrial and information ages opened the Pandora's Box of judging doctrinal positions on the basis of appeal. I believe this is what Paul foresaw when he said, *For the time will come when they will not endure sound doctrine; but after their own lusts shall they heap to themselves teachers, having itching ears; And they shall turn away their ears from the truth, and shall be turned unto fables* (2 Tim 4:3-4). I'm sure you'll notice the title for this book in the above passage.

Once error is established within a denominational hierarchy it can remain unchallenged for centuries. We no longer burn our heretics at the stake or feed them to lions, but we do still ostracize those who question church orthodoxy. It takes a tremendous amount of time, energy, and prayerful study, to build from scratch a personal systematic theology that encompasses all the major doctrines and considers *"all the counsel of God"*. It doesn't even occur to most people that they should develop their own personal systematic theology. Everyone should know what they believe, and the Biblical basis for that belief, on every point of doctrine. Ideally, everyone's theology would be the result of exhaustive research that is motivated by a love of truth, guided by prayer, and tempered by reverential fear and trembling. But that is the road less traveled. Even if one chooses not to adopt the canned doctrine passed down by the denomination, it is much easier and a lot less controversial to just leave it unchallenged.

I'd like to make one final point before moving on to specific doctrinal errors I believe the church is disseminating. This point has to do with whether or not I believe the errors are entirely random or the result of dark forces orchestrating behind the scenes. Let's consider the difference between an isolated case of taking the most appealing doctrinal interpretation and doing the same thing systematically. Let's say we fill out our complicated tax return and make twenty-three errors in the process. The IRS audits and finds that the errors seem to be pretty evenly divided between those that increase the tax liability and those that diminish it. The logical conclusion will be that no sinister motives were involved. On the other hand, if all twenty-three errors are in the preparers favor, a convincing case can be made for intentional deception. The same is true of doctrinal positions. We can all make mistakes. But when all the mistakes are on one side, the side of appeal, one must assume there is intentional deception involved. That doesn't necessarily mean the developers of the doctrinal positions were intentionally deceptive. They may not have been focused on the big picture and didn't understand all the potential ramifications of their inherent biases. Their predispositions toward more appealing doctrine may have simply been used to turn them into pawns in a deception that is taking place on a scale beyond their focus. They were dealing with the seemingly small skirmish of finding consensus on a particular doctrine, while the adversary was setting them up to lose a war in which they didn't even realize they were engaged. Such is the subtlety of the enemy.

Going back to our tax return analogy, because all the errors are on the side of "appeal", I believe forces setting the stage for the deceptions of the last days have been busy leading the church to systematically water down the hard truths. In some cases the watering down has been led by charlatans attempting to commercialize and profit from the message and in other cases it has been led by well meaning, but misguided, individuals trying to broaden the appeal of the message in order to reach more people. Unfortunately, in both cases, the people are misled. Watering down the gospel may broaden its appeal, but it can also completely negate its effectiveness for both the lost and the faithful. Water it down and the lost will find it difficult to distinguish between the true gospel and itching ears theology. Even if they manage to find salvation, a steady diet of itching ears theology will render them ineffective if they are the generation called upon to confront the master of deception, the Antichrist.

I make this point because all the doctrinal issues we'll examine in the following chapters have at least some supporting evidence on both sides. Most are weighted toward the less appealing, but some are nearly balanced. The point is not that the churches position is totally without merit in all, or any, of the cases. The point is that the church has systematically adopted the more appealing position, even when it is not supported by a preponderance of the evidence. I further believe this systematic error on the side of appeal is guided by sinister forces that run deeper than the individuals involved. In spiritual warfare, we are dealing with incredibly cunning and subtle forces that use unsuspecting people as mere pawns (Gen 3:1). It is so tempting to adopt a doctrine or position that may have less than a fifty percent chance of being accurate when it is five hundred percent more appealing. Eve may have been the first to roll the dice in this regard, but the scriptures are full of those who have fallen into this trap. As an institution, the church has fallen for this literal "oldest trick in the book". By adopting positions short on merit but long on appeal the church sold out its own credibility and unwittingly became a party to the final deception.

I am calling on the church to re-examine its doctrinal positions where the evidence warrants; acknowledge the counterpoints in all cases; and encourage all to join with the church in pursuit of ultimate truth. If we are to *endure unto the end* and be *saved* (Mt 24:12); if we are to be among the *elect* (Mt 24:24) that are not taken in by the deception; if we are to avoid spiritual death, we must become lovers of truth (2ⁿᵈ Thes 2:10), not guardians of orthodoxy. And remember, the prophets of old, for the most part, were not sent to comfort the afflicted, but rather to afflict the comfortable. It is time once again to afflict the comfortable. The church needs to heed 2ⁿᵈ Corinthians 13:5, where Paul admonished us to *"Examine yourselves, whether ye be in the faith;..."* Instead of taking offence as though it were a king that had just been insulted, the church needs to *"think soberly"* (Ro 12:3) of itself as it undertakes this self-examination.

I have one final word of caution for members as they take a second look at the church's major doctrines. Beware of what psychologist refer to as "belief persistence"; a polite way of saying people believe what they want to believe. Belief persistence is a well-known phenomenon whereby people will cling to preferred beliefs despite overwhelming evidence to the contrary. They do this by assigning a disproportionate amount of weight to the evidence that supports the position they wish to take, while discounting, or ignoring altogether, evidence that does not. You will see this over and over again as people try to defend various components of their "itching ears theology". Present them with Biblical language that seems to dispute their doctrine and the verbal gymnastics and semantics they will employ to dismiss it are almost laughable. Present them with Biblical language that is absolutely indisputable and they will fall back on "that was meant for another person at another time; it doesn't apply to us". Learn to recognize these symptoms of "belief persistence" and don't fall victim to them. The antidote for "belief persistence", as with the other obstacles to sound doctrine, is a pure love of truth. I hope that is what you take from this book.

CHAPTER TWO

"Easybelieveism"

IT'S HARD TO IMAGINE any individual today who isn't familiar with John 3:16. *For God so loved the world, that he gave his only begotten Son, that whosoever believeth in him should not perish, but have everlasting life.* In the race to win converts, grow their ministries, and / or recruit supporters, the church has been far too eager to promote this simple truth to the exclusion of the more complicated and less appealing whole truth.

The whole truth is that something more than acknowledgement is required. James put it best when he said, *Thou believest that there is one God; thou doest well: the devils also believe, and tremble.* James is not contradicting John. He is making the same point I wish to make. The belief contemplated in John 3:16 is beyond mere acknowledgement. Devils, or demons, are well aware of God and Christ. They have no doubt. Obviously, there is a difference between the belief of demons and the belief that brings salvation. It has always been incumbent on the church to differentiate between the two and make sure it is not promoting the faith of demons; mere acknowledgement. I believe the church has largely failed in this regard. It has promoted the simplest and most appealing half of the truth, while leaving out or downplaying the more critical, more complex, and less appealing half. The ingredient that must be added in order to transform the belief of demons into the belief that brings salvation is surrender. The demon isn't lacking in faith, he just has no intention of surrendering to the Lord's will. This is a hard truth that is difficult to understand or explain and even harder to swallow. The good news is salvation doesn't require that we understand the theology behind the need for surrender; it only requires that we be willing to do so. The bad news is willful surrender is contrary to human nature. We owe it to the lost to emphasize the role surrender plays in salvation. We can do our best to explain that victory follows surrender; but in the end it has to be an act of faith because the lost cannot fully comprehend or appreciate the spiritual paradox of victory through surrender.

After many years of walking with Christ, I still marvel at how victory over sin, life, death, hell, and the grave, comes by way of surrender. I have never been able to find the exact words to describe my state of mind when I decided to give up trying to bend people, places, and things to my will and surrender instead to the will of a God I wasn't sure existed. It began with the realization that my life was a spiritual train wreck. I was having some financial success, but I was a miserable human being trapped in a life of quiet desperation. I was getting through from day to day by anesthetizing myself with drugs and alcohol. In one moment, I simultaneously came to grips with several things. First, my way wasn't working. My decision to go my own way and do my own thing had not only made me miserable, it was also laying more stripes on the Christ whose suffering had already purchased for me the abundant life. For the first time, I knew what Isaiah 53:6 meant; *All we like sheep have gone astray; we have turned every one to his own way; and the LORD hath laid on him the iniquity of us all.* When that reality dawned on me, I was filled with regret and purposed in my heart to turn from my self-seeking ways. I think religions once called that repentance; another word you really don't hear much these days. It may even be more unpopular than surrender. Repentance was the frame of mind that preceded the willingness to surrender. I also remain at a loss in trying to explain the overwhelming sense of faith, peace, and liberation that came over me at the moment I truly "let go and let God". I came to the table with faith, but it wasn't saving faith. At some level I may have always acknowledged an omniscient and omnipotent God, but I had never even considered giving up the effort to manipulate my little section of the universe. Somehow, when I reached that indescribable tipping point of surrender, God took over and transformed my little kernel of belief into the miraculous faith that brings salvation.

Any teaching of saving faith that does not emphasize the role of surrender is "easybelieveism". We cannot claim Him as Savior if we haven't made Him Lord of our lives. We must surrender all. Most churches still pay lip service to this concept, but very few, if any, treat it like the lynch pin it is. We have to turn our will and our lives over to Him. That is complete surrender and the key to salvation. It's interesting that the group most accurately promoting the Biblical role of surrender in salvation is not the church; it's Alcoholics Anonymous. The first step in the program (admitted we are powerless) requires a dose of humility. Not coincidentally, this is also the first step toward salvation. The second step involves an acknowledgement of God (came to believe). And the third requires a decision to surrender our will to the will of God. Unfortunately, the church emphasizes step two almost exclusively. AA knows it's really all about step three. I don't think it's a coincidence that one will find a higher percentage of spiritually mature individuals in the ranks of AA than in the ranks of church attendees. In AA step eleven we find the ultimate result of spiritual maturity, the ability to die to self-interest and pray only for the knowledge of God's will for your life and the strength to carry that out. Again, Christ set the example with His prayer in Gethsemane; "*not my will, but thine, be done*".

I also don't think it's a coincidence that AA has remained focused on the core of what's required for a spiritual rebirth while the church became distracted. There is a perfectly good reason for the difference. Unlike the church, AA is structured in such a way that no one profits from increased attendance. Accordingly, there has been no effort to make the message more appealing by de-emphasizing surrender.

The church's lack of emphasis on surrender today has led it to count among its supporters a lot of people who have simply acknowledged God and are going through the requisite religious rituals in the hope that it will save them. They are stuck on AA's step two. They may think their acknowledgement of God places them among the "*whosoever believeth*", but without surrender, they may be relying on the faith of demons. They may have even made a public profession of faith, but faith can be feigned or confused with acknowledgement. They may have confessed their sins, but without genuine repentance and surrender, a confession is of no avail. Without a contrite heart, a confession is just a string of connected words. Many a huckster has made a tearful confession when caught with his hand in the cookie jar. In many cases it is just an attempt to keep the donations flowing. Surrender is the key. When we add the ingredient of surrender to our acknowledgement of God, He, not us, supernaturally transforms mere knowledge into saving faith. It's a spiritual transformation only God can handle. Paul made this point when he said in Eph 2:8 *For by grace are ye saved through faith; and that not of yourselves: it is the gift of God.* We can take no credit for even the faith that saves us. It is imparted to us when we add the ingredient of surrender to our knowledge of the gospel. Acknowledgment and a willingness to surrender is all we bring to the table. Acknowledgment alone, public or private, is not enough. Implying that it is, or even allowing people to believe that it is, constitutes "easybelieveism".

There appears to be a classic example of "easybelieveism" in Acts 8:5-25, with particular emphasis on verses 13 through 25. In verse 13 we find that a man named Simon "*believed*" and "*was baptized*"; then "*continued with Phillip*". But when he saw a commercial opportunity related to his previous employment and reminiscent of today's televangelist (verses 18-21), he succumbed to his lust for money. We will never know if Simon's initial belief was mere acknowledgment, also known as the "faith of demons", or if he was genuinely saved. It does seem clear that he was not sufficiently surrendered to the Lord's will. It would appear the resulting rebuke from Phillip may have put him back on the straight and narrow. The point is that the whole episode raises legitimate questions related to both the doctrines of "easybelieveism" and "eternal security".

If Simon, in Acts 8:5-25, is a classic example of being insufficiently surrendered, the three Hebrew children known as Meshach, Shadrach, and Abednego are classic examples of ultimate surrender. You will no doubt recall that when they were threatened with being thrown into the fiery furnace for not bowing to an idol and were asked the rhetorical question by the king, *"and who is that God that shall deliver you out of my hands?"* (Daniel 3:15). They responded with *"we are not careful to answer thee in this matter, If it be so, our God whom we serve is able to deliver us from the burning fiery furnace, and he will deliver us out of thine hand, O king. But **if not**, be it known unto thee, O king, that we will not serve thy gods, nor worship the golden image..."* (Daniel 3:16-18). In modern parlance, they were saying, this is a no brainer; God is able to deliver us and He will deliver us, one way or another; but our decision to do what we believe is right is not contingent on what God may, or may not, choose to do. Notice the "if not" in verse 18. They had no crystal ball. They expected to be delivered either through death or supernatural intervention. They were leaving it up to God to decide which. The essence of surrender is acknowledging His lordship and putting your life in His hands. This is the level of surrender the church should be promoting. Life is always going to present us with "ifs" and "if nots". The properly surrendered saint, like the 3 Hebrew children, is able to deal with either on an even keel.

All this discussion about degrees of belief can make the salvation process seem very complicated, esoteric, and convoluted to the lost, but in reality, it is but a one step process, surrender. The appearance of complexity and the paradox of victory by surrender are just two of the ways God hid His plan from the "wise and prudent while revealing it unto babes" In Matthew 11:25 Christ himself thanks God *"because thou hast hid these things from the wise and prudent, and has revealed them unto babes."* Children are predisposed to belief in the supernatural and they are already dependent on, and subservient to, the will of others. The idea of surrender to a Higher Power is not such an obstacle to a child. The wise and prudent on the other hand are accustomed to getting by on intellect and self-sufficiency. It's not that intellectuals can't get to heaven; it's just that God made sure the Albert Einsteins of the world would have no advantage over the Forrest Gumps when it came to salvation. To level the playing field, He negated their intellectual advantage by making humility and surrender proportionately more difficult for them. The first step toward heaven isn't aptitude, it's attitude. The formula for saving faith is simultaneously both profoundly simple and impossibly complex.

But enough with the theory, what are the mechanics of making something so simple a child can stumble upon it and simultaneously so esoteric that even a genius can't figure it out. Exactly how does One hide spiritual truths from a mature, educated, intellectual, while revealing them to the immature and uneducated? It's done by hiding them in plain view, under shrouds of parables, allegories, metaphors, and paradoxes? Even if the intellectual correctly interprets some of the parables, allegories, and metaphors, and manages to peel back a few of the layers, he'll keep confronting paradoxes. A paradox, by definition, is a concept that appears self-contradictory. The path to spiritual enlightenment is full of them. We worship a suffering messiah. We have to surrender to win. We die to live. And we suffer to get well; just to name a few. Each paradox the intellectual trying to rationalize his way to salvation confronts will convince him he has gotten off the path by misconstruing a parable, allegory, or metaphor somewhere along the way. This new doubt reinforces the doubt that led to the analytical approach in the first place. I think this is referred to as a negative feedback loop. Regardless of how often he takes up the challenge, or how many variations of the original thought processes he tries, he'll never be comfortable with conclusions that appear self-contradictory. He will remain mired in doubt and unwilling to surrender. He will also remain lost until he is able to approach the throne of grace with a contrite and humble spirit. I can't say it better than Psalm 34:18, *The LORD is nigh unto them that are of a broken heart; and saveth such as be of a contrite spirit.*

No person ever reasoned their way to salvation. The most profound spiritual truths are beyond the reach of pure reason. They cannot be extracted by intellect alone. As Paul said in 1st Cor 2:14 ...*the natural man receiveth not the things of the Spirit of God: for they are foolishness unto him: neither can he know them, because they are spiritually discerned.* Think of the path to spiritual enlightenment as a stairway to heaven (seems like an appropriate analogy). On the lowest section of the stairway are truths one can grasp visually and intellectually. The Bible refers to these truths in Romans 1:20 when it says that all of creation gives testimony to the existence of God, so that everyone is without excuse. Our consciences also bear witness (Ro 2:15). Everyone can see God's handiwork throughout the universe, and most will even acknowledge it as such. But this is carnal knowledge, not saving faith. It will only take you a few steps up the stairway. The truths beyond the purview of the carnal mind are behind a Door. Jesus Christ is that Door. The Door to salvation is opened when we come to believe and surrender to His will for our lives. Only then do we have access to the spiritually discerned truths that can lead to full enlightenment. The sinner, whether it be an Albert Einstein or a Forrest Gump, who shows up at the Door in the right frame of mind will find the Door to salvation wide open and the spiritual truths on the other side will be revealed as though a blindfold has been removed. The sinner who shows up in the wrong frame of mind will find that no amount of raw intellect or carnal knowledge will open the Door. Far too often, the "wise and prudent" arrive at the Door armed with knowledge and intellect, determined to pry it open and extract the truth.

The reason salvation is a spiritual experience and not a mechanical process is that "surrender" is not just step three in a three part process; it is a state of mind. First, we have to acknowledge our own limitations to realize the need for a Savior. Second, we have to believe there is a Savior. Third, we have to surrender to His will for our lives. Although it involves steps, these are not mechanical processes. Prescribed words cannot be strung together in some pre-determined order as though one were following an algebraic formula. One can recite "the sinner's prayer" as though it were a mantra until they are blue in the face, and if the heart is not right, it will not bring salvation. Surrender, and the salvation it brings, is a state of mind, born of humility, and a contrite heart and spirit. Unfortunately, the modern church places all the emphasis on the formula ("the sinner's prayer") because it is uniform, simple, and easy. The result is a church full of nominal believers that know nothing of the power, peace, or joy that surrender brings. They may go through the rituals of church attendance and participate in church programs, but they are acting out of self-will and in pursuit of self-interest. They are making themselves do it because they don't want to go to hell; or perhaps church is their social life. I believe Jesus is referring to these nominal believers when he said; *"Not every one that saith unto me, Lord, Lord, shall enter into the kingdom of heaven; but he that doeth the will of my Father which is in heaven. Many will say to me in that day, Lord, Lord, have we not prophesied in thy name? and in thy name have cast out devils? and in thy name done many wonderful works? And then will I profess unto them, I never knew you: depart from me, ye that work iniquity."* (Mt 7:21-23) Notice the phrase *"will of my Father"*. God doesn't want our *"many wonderful works"* if they are motivated by self-will. He wants us totally surrendered to God so all of our *"works"*, everything we do, is an expression of *"the will of my Father"*. He doesn't want us setting aside certain times of the day or week for *"works"*; He wants us walking in His will every moment of every day. In the end, our activities might be much the same, but the driving force behind them will be different.

"Rich" people might have an even harder time with surrender than the "wise and prudent". Remember Jesus' teaching in this regard; *"It is easier for a camel to go through the eye of a needle, than for a rich man to enter into the kingdom of God."* (Mark 10:25) The rich know that surrendering their lives also means surrendering the riches that may have been accumulated over a lifetime, or even generations. They may not be called upon to disperse their wealth, but they must be willing to do so. It couldn't be easy, but it is not impossible. I should note that Jesus' statement was a bit of obvious hyperbole. Yes, that's right; there are no errors in the Bible, but hyperbole was often used to drive home a point. It is a very effective literary tool. We find it throughout the Old Testament. An excellent example is Joshua 7:12; *"And the Midianites and the Amalekites and all the children of the east lay along in the valley like grasshoppers for multitude; and their camels were without number, as the sand by the sea side for multitude."* Other examples in the New Testament include Jesus talking about the "blind" leading the "blind" in reference to the Pharisees and their straining gnats while swallowing camels. Clearly, they did not swallow camels and they weren't literally blind. What they did was obsess about trivial matters while failing to see the big picture. We shouldn't fall into the same trap. We are expected to glean the point from the text without taking it literally. Salvation is humanly impossible for both rich and poor; it takes an act of God. The surrender state of mind that sets the stage for it is contrary to human nature and especially difficult for a rich person that is more likely to be accustomed to imposing his own will on situations. But, if we are willing to surrender to God, He can change our hearts and our minds in the twinkling of an eye. Jesus makes this point a couple of verses later in Mark 10:27; *"And Jesus looking upon them saith, With men it is impossible, but not with God: for with God all things are possible."*

I know the unenlightened are turned off by the concept of surrender. I know most of them are laboring under the illusion that if they surrender to God's will for their lives, they'll have to take a vow of poverty and end up on a mission field having to worry about being eaten by cannibals. It is difficult to explain how God uses most of us on missions within our own families and communities. For some, their whole "mission" in life might be to inspire someone else to greatness. Who knows what life well lived or word rightly spoken will inspire the next Martin Luther or Billy Graham. We're all commissioned to spread the gospel, but it is entirely appropriate for the work to begin at home. Anyone who has raised a God fearing child or two has achieved a great mission in life.

In summary; surrendering to the Lord's will for our lives won't land us all in a fiery furnace or on a mission field, but surrender we must. I can't say it enough; the church does a disservice to the gospel, the church, and the lost, when it promotes a form of "easybelieveism" by failing to emphasize the vital role of surrender in salvation. A believer insufficiently surrendered will not be able to withstand the kind of tribulation many past Christians have already endured, and future Christians are promised. Instead of raising an army of spiritual warriors willing to martyr themselves for the cause of Christ, the church is collecting a group of nominal believers that will "fall away" from the faith when the persecution of the saints begins. In the general sense, this can't be prevented. The Bible predicts it will happen and therefore it must come to pass. However, as individuals, we can choose not to be among the fallen.

The Bible teaches about a belief that saves and a belief that doesn't. The difference is surrender. Unfortunately, more often than not, the church is teaching the wrong version.

CHAPTER THREE

"Eternal Security"

THE DOCTRINE OF ETERNAL security in its simplest form is the belief that "once saved, always saved". When one considers "*all the counsel of God*" there is virtually no Biblical basis for this doctrine. Likewise there is no basis for the doctrine in early church history. The church had been around for nearly 1600 years before John Calvin introduced the concept. Even then it was more or less confined to a debate among theologians for the next 300 years. It took the modern era of televangelism to spread the doctrine of eternal security throughout Christendom. To be sure, there are a number of scriptures one can cite in isolation to support this doctrine. However, none are definitive and they are overwhelmed by a much larger number of unequivocal passages that point to people retaining their free will and being able to turn their backs on God, even after they have been redeemed. Because so many passages are open to different interpretations, it is impossible to assign a precise number to the quantity of passages that support the Arminian position that a person, once saved, may be lost again. However, even Calvinist would probably admit there are dozens. My professors at the Liberty Bible Institute, a school steeped in the Calvinist tradition, acknowledged the Arminian position was not without Biblical support. To their considerable credit, they freely admitted there may be as many as one hundred supporting passages. Their thorough and fair presentation of a position contrary to their own is a testament to both the merits of the argument and the integrity of the people. It also speaks well of the institution that the presentation of competing ideas is condoned.

I believe the strongest verse in support of the Calvinist position of once saved always saved is John 10:28 *²⁸And I give unto them eternal life; and they shall never perish, neither shall any man pluck them out of my hand.* Of course Arminians would certainly acknowledge that God's gift of eternal life is freely given to all and those who accept and continue in the faith "shall never perish". However, some will not accept. Others will accept and later turn their backs on God. It's true that no one can pluck us out of God's hand. But nothing in this passage precludes one from walking away of his own free will. It seems counterintuitive that the God who purposefully gave us a free will would take it back upon redemption.

Many Calvinist believe Romans 8:30 is the most convincing verse in the Bible on the doctrine of eternal security. Romans 8:30 reads *³⁰Moreover whom he did predestinate, them he also called: and whom he called, them he also justified: and whom he justified, them he also glorified.* The Calvinist is likely to suggest that because glorified is in the past tense, it means that upon getting saved, a person is already glorified in heaven and that is irreversible. I see the passage differently. Since all the verbs in the verse are past tense, I believe it is more a lesson in the omniscience and timelessness of God than it is a lesson in eternal security. I see no contextual evidence this verse was intended as a lesson in eternal security. I don't think it can be interpreted as such unless it is also interpreted as a proof of predestination. Both doctrines are far too significant to be drawn from isolated passages of questionable intent. Without getting bogged down in the debate over predestination, I believe Paul's point is that God is timeless. We see time unfolding in a linear fashion from start to finish. God has seen all and known all from the beginning. Considering that God has complete foreknowledge of all events, past, present, and future, we are predestined, called, justified, and glorified, only to the extent that He foreknew we would make and follow through on a commitment to surrender to His will. If not, He would foreknow that we would make a decision to turn our backs on Him and we would be relegated to the role of a Judas or Pilate.

People (including myself) holding the Arminian position that a person, once saved, retains the right to turn away from God and forfeit his salvation, are fond of quoting from 2nd Peter. In Chapter 2 and Verse 4 we find, *For if God spared not the angels that sinned, but cast them down to hell, and delivered them into chains of darkness, to be reserved unto judgment...* In verses 20 through 22 we find, *20For if after they have escaped the pollutions of the world through the knowledge of the Lord and Saviour Jesus Christ, they are again entangled therein, and overcome, the latter end is worse with them than the beginning. 21For it had been better for them not to have known the way of righteousness, than, after they have known it, to turn from the holy commandment delivered unto them. 22But it is happened unto them according to the true proverb, The dog is turned to his own vomit again; and the sow that was washed to her wallowing in the mire.* Unlike the verses cited above in defense of the "once saved always saved" Calvinist position, these verses are specifically aimed at teaching on the subject at hand. It is a notice and a warning for those who have *"escaped the pollutions of the world through the knowledge of the Lord and Saviour Jesus Christ"* and *"are again entangled therein"*.

The "once saved always saved" Calvinist like to say these later verses of 2nd Peter don't apply to us. They say Peter is speaking of false prophets that were never saved in the first place. This is a specious argument at best. It is based on something they can't possibly know (the status of another's salvation). It unnecessarily limits the application of the text. It cuts against the clear language of the text. And conveniently for them, it cannot be subjected to proofs. Even if one accepts this argument as it relates to the later verses of 2nd Peter Chapter 2, I don't see how the argument can be applied to the angels in verse 4. When we read verse 4, *For if God spared not the angels that sinned, but cast them down to hell, and delivered them into chains of darkness, to be reserved unto judgment...*, it seems clear that the whole point of the passage is that God will let even angels retain the free will to turn their backs on Him. And if they so choose, He will cast them out accordingly. After all, isn't Lucifer himself a fallen angel? How does one acknowledge on the one hand that God will cast out and send to hell even those who have risen to the status of angel, while on the other hand insisting that a mere mortal can do nothing to forfeit their salvation? Such would seem to be the "once saved always saved" Calvinist position.

I believe that maintaining the "once saved always saved" position in the face of the above passage in 2nd Peter is a clear example of "belief persistence"; the irrational clinging to a desirable belief even in the face of overwhelming evidence to the contrary. The Calvinist can't say the language isn't clear. They are relegated to the defense that it doesn't apply to us. They are taking the position that it may apply to angels and false prophets, but we can draw no lessons from it!

As we go through the various arguments and counter-arguments relating to these questionable doctrines, you'll see that the "itching ears theologians" have to repeatedly invoke the "that doesn't apply to us" argument. That's because in most cases the language is so clear, the only way they can maintain their position is to set aside whole sections of scripture. I think all of us should be rightfully skeptical any time the "doesn't apply to us" argument is invoked to set aside specific instructions from the New Testament. The Bible is clear, *All scripture is given by inspiration of God, and is profitable for doctrine, for reproof, for correction, for instruction in righteousness* (2nd Timothy 3:16). If we can set aside vast inconvenient swatches by invoking the "it doesn't apply to us" argument, is there any part of it that is sacred? After all, very little, if any of it, is written to "us" specifically. Romans was written to the Romans. Corinthians was written to the believers in Corinth. Timothy was written to Timothy. I could go on, but you get the point. We can't choose to disregard passages just because they are not specifically addressed to us. Yet there are those who would disregard passages from the Bible on the basis that the text was not addressed to us, then turn around and offer a passage from the same category of text to support their position.

While the above referenced verses in 2nd Peter are the strongest in favor of the saved retaining their free will; I'd like to cite a few more that, if taken at face value, would dispel the notion of "once saved, always saved".

1st Timothy 4:1 (KJV)

^{1}Now the Spirit speaketh expressly, that in the latter times some shall depart from the faith, giving heed to seducing spirits, and doctrines of devils;

I know we can look at 1st Timothy 4:1 and begin with the mental and verbal gymnastics, or resort to the "it doesn't apply to us" argument, but I prefer to take the position that it means just what it says; some will depart from the faith as the result of being taken in by seducing spirits and doctrines of devils. The ideas of "easybelieveism", "eternal security", "prosperity theology", "escapeism", etc. can all be very seductive. Weave them together with a few lesser known doctrinal errors and you have "itching ears theology". It tends to give the listener a warm fuzzy feeling, but its scriptural basis is dubious at best.

Colossians 1:21-23(KJV)

^{21}And you, that were sometime alienated and enemies in your mind by wicked works, yet now hath he reconciled
^{22}In the body of his flesh through death, to present you holy and unblameable and unreproveable in his sight:
^{23}If ye continue in the faith grounded and settled, and be not moved away from the hope of the gospel, which ye have heard, and which was preached to every creature which is under heaven; whereof I Paul am made a minister;

In this passage Paul notes that we have been reconciled to God by the sacrifice of Jesus Christ *If ye continue in the faith grounded and settled, and be not moved away from the hope of the gospel...* This text seems so self-evident, I'm afraid people will take offense at being told what it means. It is one of many verses on the subject of salvation that uses some variation of the phrase "*if ye continue*". We're going to examine the most relevant ones. Clearly, there is some threshold of commitment and endurance envisioned here. It involves more than a "once and done" verbal recitation of some typical "sinners prayer".

1 Corinthians 15:1-2(KJV)

¹Moreover, brethren, I declare unto you the gospel which I preached unto you, which also ye have received, and wherein ye stand;
²By which also ye are saved, if ye keep in memory what I preached unto you, unless ye have believed in vain.

Again, you can try to explain it away if you will, but the clear implication in verse two is that we must continue in faith in order to realize ultimate salvation. Consistent with this theme and the "faith of demons", the last phrase makes it clear that it is possible to believe in vain.

John 8:31(KJV)

³¹Then said Jesus to those Jews which believed on him, If ye continue in my word, then are ye my disciples indeed;

Here's that troublesome (for the "once saved always saved" Calvinist) word "if" and that troublesome phrase "if ye continue". One would think the continual re-emergence of that word and phrase, or words of like import, would give the Calvinist pause.

Hebrews 3:12-19(KJV)

¹²Take heed, brethren, lest there be in any of you an evil heart of unbelief, in departing from the living God.
¹³But exhort one another daily, while it is called To day; lest any of you be hardened through the deceitfulness of sin.
¹⁴For we are made partakers of Christ, if we hold the beginning of our confidence stedfast unto the end;
¹⁵While it is said, To day if ye will hear his voice, harden not your hearts, as in the provocation.
¹⁶For some, when they had heard, did provoke: howbeit not all that came out of Egypt by Moses.
¹⁷But with whom was he grieved forty years? was it not with them that had sinned, whose carcases fell in the wilderness?

[18]And to whom sware he that they should not enter into his rest, but to them that believed not?
[19]So we see that they could not enter in because of unbelief.

Here the writer is drawing a parallel between the waxing and waning of the faith of God's chosen people collectively and the same ebb and flow of the faith of individuals. Take particular note of verse 14; *"For we are made partakers of Christ, if we hold the beginning of our confidence stedfast unto the end;"*. Folks, I didn't add the phrase *"if we hold the beginning of our confidence stedfast unto the end"*. I don't see how it can be ignored or explained away. I don't know why a student of scripture and seeker of truth would want to explain it away. The persistent effort to do so displays a tendency to mold the scripture to one's doctrine instead of molding one's doctrine to the scripture. With all due deference to differing opinions, the origin of any doctrine that is based on one or two nebulous passages and requires the explaining away of dozens of passages that seem to clearly contradict it, is suspect.

Acts 14:22(KJV)
[22]Confirming the souls of the disciples, and exhorting them to continue in the faith, and that we must through much tribulation enter into the kingdom of God.

It would seem that if we are "once saved always saved", the repeated exhortations to "continue" in the faith would be rather superfluous. Also take note of the phrase *"we must through much tribulation enter into the kingdom of God."* This will come up again and again in the chapter on "escapeism".

1 John 2:24-25(KJV)
[24]Let that therefore abide in you, which ye have heard from the beginning. If that which ye have heard from the beginning shall remain in you, ye also shall continue in the Son, and in the Father.
[25]And this is the promise that he hath promised us, even eternal life.

Verse 25 assures us that the topic under discussion is eternal life, i.e. salvation. In that specific context we find the phrase *"If that which* ye have heard from the beginning shall remain in you, ye also shall continue in the Son". I keep reading these passages and it gets harder and harder to remain sensitive to the "once saved always saved" position. Apart from a case of pathological "belief persistence", I just don't see how one can read all these passages and maintain the Calvinist position.

Ezekiel 3:20(KJV)
20 Again, When a righteous man doth turn from his righteousness, and commit iniquity, and I lay a stumblingblock before him, he shall die: because thou hast not given him warning, he shall die in his sin, and his righteousness which he hath done shall not be remembered; but his blood will I require at thine hand.

In this passage we find that not only does a person have the free will to "*turn from his righteousness*" and thereby "*die in his sin*" with his previous righteousness forgotten, but furthermore, anyone who does not avail themselves of an opportunity to warn the individual will also be called to account for the loss.

Revelation 22:19(KJV)
19 And if any man shall take away from the words of the book of this prophecy, God shall take away his part out of the book of life, and out of the holy city, and from the things which are written in this book.

This verse provides more evidence that a person's name can be erased from the book of life. How else would one explain "*God shall take away his part out of the book of life*"? Upon reading this verse, it seems to me that even the staunchest "once saved always saved" Calvinist would have to acknowledge there are circumstances whereby a person might forfeit their salvation.

Hebrews 6:4-6(KJV)
4 For it is impossible for those who were once enlightened, and have tasted of the heavenly gift, and were made partakers of the Holy Ghost, 5 And have tasted the good word of God, and the powers of the world to come,

⁶If they shall fall away, to renew them again unto repentance; seeing they crucify to themselves the Son of God afresh, and put him to an open shame.

It is much easier to comprehend the truncated version of these verses. Take the first phrase of verse 4 and place it before verse 6 and it reads like this; *⁴For it is impossible for those who were once enlightened, ⁶If they shall fall away, to renew them again unto repentance; seeing they crucify to themselves the Son of God afresh, and put him to an open shame.* Not only does this seem to blow the doctrine of "eternal security" out of the water, but it also suggests one can reach a height of enlightenment from which a fall is eternally fatal. Perhaps this is the height from which Lucifer and his minions fell. This would explain why redemption does not appear to be an option for them.

Hebrews 10:26(KJV)
²⁶For if we sin wilfully after that we have received the knowledge of the truth, there remaineth no more sacrifice for sins,

This seems to tie in with the previous passage (Heb 6:4-6). It is a "hard saying". It seems to suggest that one that has "received the knowledge of the truth" can reject the ways of God to such an extent that atonement might be difficult, or impossible, to find.

2 John 1:8(KJV)
⁸Look to yourselves, that we lose not those things which we have wrought, but that we receive a full reward.

Apparently people had crept into this early church denying that Christ had come in the flesh. The writer is telling us we can lose what we have gained if we are seduced by the deniers of Christ. The "once saved always saved" Calvinist will say this potential loss only applies to rewards in heaven, not the ticket to heaven itself. I could concede that this applies to rewards, but it must be noted that the ticket to heaven itself is one of the rewards of salvation. There is no limit placed here on the extent of rewards that are subject to loss if we turn our backs on Christ.

1 Corinthians 9:27(KJV)

²⁷But I keep under my body, and bring it into subjection: lest that by any means, when I have preached to others, I myself should be a castaway.

A straightforward reading of this passage seems to indicate that the Apostle Paul didn't even consider himself exempt from becoming one of God's castaways if he should decide to turn his back on the ways of God.

Matthew 5:13(KJV)

¹³Ye are the salt of the earth: but if the salt have lost his savour, wherewith shall it be salted? it is thenceforth good for nothing, but to be cast out, and to be trodden under foot of men.

This excerpt, taken from the Sermon On The Mount, seems to suggest that we will be cast out if we cease to function as a preservative and a light unto the rest of the world. The Calvinist can quibble about the extent of this "casting out", but I wouldn't want to bet eternal life on "casting out" meaning something less than salvation lost.

2 Peter 1:10(KJV)

¹⁰Wherefore the rather, brethren, give diligence to make your calling and election sure: for if ye do these things, ye shall never fall:

Apparently "falling" is an option. Again, we can quibble about what is meant by "fall", but at some point it would seem that the Calvinist would just give up quibbling and at least acknowledge that "falling", in every sense, is at least a possibility. After all, for most of us "fall" is not a difficult word. If one finds himself having to endlessly parse even simple words and passages in order to defend a preferred belief, it may be time to let the language mean what it says and re-evaluate the belief. This sounds easy, but for a lot of people, "belief persistence" has reached the point of delusion.

1 Thessalonians 3:5(KJV)

⁵For this cause, when I could no longer forbear, I sent to know your faith, lest by some means the tempter have tempted you, and our labour be in vain.

I freely confess, that in terms of its implications for being able to lose one's salvation, this verse can be explained away. The question that begs is; why do Calvinist persist in their desire to explain so many verses away? Are they motivated by a love of truth, or perhaps a desire to preserve a doctrine that gives them a warm fuzzy?

1 Timothy 1:19-20(KJV)

[19] Holding faith, and a good conscience; which some having put away concerning faith have made shipwreck:
[20] Of whom is Hymenaeus and Alexander; whom I have delivered unto Satan, that they may learn not to blaspheme.

I understand this passage is not conclusive because of some ambiguity in the language, but the phrase "having put away concerning faith" does indicate once again that the faith that saved us can be put away and the result is shipwreck. It is also interesting in the sense that Paul mentions culprits by name and indicates that he has delivered them unto Satan. This may seem a bit harsh, but I assume Paul was justified.

Romans 11:20-22(KJV)

[20] Well; because of unbelief they were broken off, and thou standest by faith. Be not highminded, but fear:
[21] For if God spared not the natural branches, take heed lest he also spare not thee.
[22] Behold therefore the goodness and severity of God: on them which fell, severity; but toward thee, goodness, if thou continue in his goodness: otherwise thou also shalt be cut off.

In this passage Paul uses the analogy of an olive tree having branches cut off and other branches grafted in their place. The Jews who rejected Christ are represented by the branches that are being cut off for unbelief. The Gentiles are being grafted in for their faith. In the same breath Paul cautions the Gentiles about getting high minded and warns that they can be cut off also if they fail to *"continue in his goodness"*. There are those words again "if" and "continue" The "once saved always saved" Calvinist would say Paul is talking collectively of the Jews and Gentiles, and suggest the passage has no application to an individual's salvation. My response of course is what do you mean there is no application to the individual? What are Jews and Gentiles but a collection of individuals?

The generalization that the Jews rejected Christ and the Gentiles accepted Him is only true in a general sense. As individuals, there were many Jews who believed and many Gentiles who didn't. Whether individual Jew or individual Gentile, when they came to believe they were grafted in as individuals, irrespective of the group with which they were associated. How then can the Calvinist maintain that this passage has no application to an individual's being grafted in or cut off? This is another example of a passage so clear in its language, the Calvinist wish to dismiss it on the basis that it doesn't apply to us. Once again, I must say, if we dismiss all the passages that aren't specifically addressed to us, there won't be anything left. The portions of the Bible that aren't a history of the Jews and Gentiles are a collection of letters to the Ephesians, Thessalonians, Romans, Philippians, Corinthians, etc. None of the books are addressed to me, my city, state, or country. That doesn't mean I shouldn't draw lessons from them and it doesn't give me the right to "cherry pick" the ones that fit my preferred theology and dismiss the rest.

1st Samuel Chapters 10-31 Obviously this is not a simple passage of scripture, but rather a story about the first king of Israel, Saul. I chose him because the Bible sheds some light on his spiritual condition at two stages of his life. This is important because we cannot know the status of an individual's salvation unless it is illuminated by scripture. In 1st Samuel chapter 10 we find several verses that strongly suggest Saul was a saved believer. In verse 6 Samuel the prophet tells Saul "*the Spirit of the Lord will come upon thee*" and you "*shalt be turned into another man*". In verse 7, Samuel tells him "*God is with thee*". In verse 9 we learn "*And it was so, that when he had turned his back to go from Samuel, God gave him another heart…*". In verse 10 we find the language, "*and the Spirit of God came upon him,…*" It is difficult to read these comments and maintain the position that Saul was unsaved at this point.

In subsequent chapters it seems that Saul begins to depart from the specific instructions of God and rely more on his own judgment. Dare we say, as he became less surrendered he became less saved? In chapter 15 verses 2 and 3, Saul is specifically instructed; *²Thus saith the LORD of hosts, I remember that which Amalek did to Israel, how he laid wait for him in the way, when he came up from Egypt. ³Now go and smite Amalek, and utterly destroy all that they have, and spare them not; but slay both man and woman, infant and suckling, ox and sheep, camel and ass.* In verse 9, we learn that Saul did not carry out his instructions; *⁹But Saul and the people spared Agag, and the best of the sheep, and of the oxen, and of the fatlings, and the lambs, and all that was good, and would not utterly destroy them: but every thing that was vile and refuse, that they destroyed utterly.* When the prophet Samuel confronted him about his disobedience (15:17-19), Saul was defensive and argumentative, suggesting that the spoils were taken to be offered as a sacrifice unto God (15:20-21). Samuel's famous response is found in verses 22-23; *And Samuel said, Hath the LORD as great delight in burnt offerings and sacrifices, as in obeying the voice of the LORD? Behold, to obey is better than sacrifice, and to hearken than the fat of rams. ²³For rebellion is as the sin of witchcraft, and stubbornness is as iniquity and idolatry. Because thou hast rejected the word of the LORD, he hath also rejected thee from being king.* In short, obedience/surrender is God's objective for us and rebellion is the opposite. In Chapter 16 verse 14 we find *¹⁴But the Spirit of the LORD departed from Saul, and an evil spirit from the LORD troubled him.* There is much more in subsequent chapters about the troubled remainder of Saul's life, but suffice to say, his rebellion resulted in the loss of the relationship he clearly had with God. We know the Spirit of God departed from him and God stopped answering his prayers. The Calvinist can quibble about the extent of that loss, but if the quibbling is just to preserve a doctrine for which they have a personal preference, I don't believe it behooves them to do so.

Matthew 13:3-8(KJV)

³And he spake many things unto them in parables, saying, Behold, a sower went forth to sow;

⁴And when he sowed, some seeds fell by the way side, and the fowls came and devoured them up:
⁵Some fell upon stony places, where they had not much earth: and forthwith they sprung up, because they had no deepness of earth:
⁶And when the sun was up, they were scorched; and because they had no root, they withered away.
⁷And some fell among thorns; and the thorns sprung up, and choked them:
⁸But other fell into good ground, and brought forth fruit, some an hundredfold, some sixtyfold, some thirtyfold.

Jesus explains His own parable thusly a few verses later:

Matthew 13:18-23(KJV)
¹⁸Hear ye therefore the parable of the sower.
¹⁹When any one heareth the word of the kingdom, and understandeth it not, then cometh the wicked one, and catcheth away that which was sown in his heart. This is he which received seed by the way side.
²⁰But he that received the seed into stony places, the same is he that heareth the word, and anon with joy receiveth it;
²¹Yet hath he not root in himself, but dureth for a while: for when tribulation or persecution ariseth because of the word, by and by he is offended.
²²He also that received seed among the thorns is he that heareth the word; and the care of this world, and the deceitfulness of riches, choke the word, and he becometh unfruitful.
²³But he that received seed into the good ground is he that heareth the word, and understandeth it; which also beareth fruit, and bringeth forth, some an hundredfold, some sixty, some thirty.

The "once saved always saved" Calvinist will conveniently say that only members of the fourth group (verse 23) were ever saved in the first place. This is their mantra. Because it is not subject to proof, it allows them to dismiss any and all examples of salvation apparently lost.

As it relates to this parable the Calvinists suggest that only those who endured long enough to bear fruit were every really saved. That is certainly one way to look at it; but it can't be proven without engaging in circular reasoning. The Calvinist seems to be saying that if you're ever saved, you can't be unsaved; therefore anyone who falls wasn't really saved in the first place. That is circular reasoning at its worst. It uses the conclusion that's based on the theory to prove the theory the conclusion is based on. If you take away the circular reasoning; it seems pretty clear that the people under consideration had attained some level of enlightenment / salvation. Verses 20 through 22 tell us they received the word joyfully and endured for a while; but tribulation, persecution, and worldly concerns choked out the things of God. A simple unbiased reading of the parable seems to suggest they had attained a level of salvation short of total enlightenment; a level which can be lost by one who is not deeply rooted in the ways of God. However, in the end, I don't consider this passage the "smoking gun" that killed "once saved always saved" because neither the Calvinist nor the Arminians will ever know for certain if the people under consideration were saved. I include the passage as another example of passages the Calvinist are willing to dismiss. I also include it for its implications as it relates to two other points I wish to make.

The first point is that the same people who argue passionately that the people under consideration here were never saved in the first place because they hadn't met the endurance or fruit test were probably the same people who rejected the notion that there is an endurance or fruit test as it relates to salvation when we were on the subject of "easybelieveism". Remember the premise of the "easybelieveism" camp is that "*whosoever believeth*" is not subject to qualifiers. If you accept the Calvinist argument that the people in verses 20 through 22 were not saved, this passage is perhaps a better argument than James 2:19 (*Thou believest that there is one God; thou doest well: the devils also believe, and tremble*) that a lot more than acknowledgement is required for salvation.

While I remain of the opinion that the people of Matthew 13:20 through 22 were saved and lost their way, I'll move on to the second point I wish to make about this passage; a point related to the main thesis of this book.

I believe the church of today is largely comprised of the group described in Matthew 13:20. They heard the word and with joy received it. They have acknowledged God; but due to "itching ears theology", they have no concept of the level of surrender required to transform acknowledgement into saving faith. This group goes through the motions of church attendance as a form of "fire insurance". This is the "wayside" or "stony ground" group.

The largest segment of the church is probably saved, but stunted in their growth by the entanglements of the world. They were sown and grow among the "thorns" (Mt 13:22). They are barely clinging to salvation themselves. Since they differ only slightly from the world they are called to reach, they are in no position to bear fruit. They are entangled, consumed, and choked by competing interest. Their prospects for survival are precarious. If growing conditions are good, they might survive all the way to harvest. They may even bear a little fruit before they are choked out by competing thorns. On the other hand, if they encounter drought, flood, wind, or other calamity, their roots might prove too shallow to survive.

Continuing the farming analogy, their chances of survival are greatly improved if they are cultivated. Cultivation is accomplished by running multiple "V" shaped cultivators between the rows of the young crop. The process is designed to uproot and plow under any weeds between the rows that might compete with or choke out the desired crop. The crop might experience some trauma and a temporary setback as a result of this process, but it benefits in the long run by the tamping down of competing interest. I see the role of this book as cultivating the crop of believers that make up this largest segment of the church. This group's spiritual growth is being stunted by the "itching ears theology" expressed in doctrines designed for appeal. The charlatans that lead some of today's largest churches use the enhanced appeal of these designer doctrines to attract the saints they need to fleece in order to support their lavish "ministries". This is what the Bible would call "making merchandise" of the saints. In 2nd Peter 2:1 through 3 we find; *¹But there were false prophets also among the people, even as there shall be false teachers among you, who privily shall bring in damnable heresies, even denying the Lord that bought them, and bring upon themselves swift destruction, ²And many shall follow their pernicious ways; by reason of whom the way of truth shall be evil spoken of. ³And through covetousness shall they with feigned words make merchandise of you:...*

The charlatans who would *"make merchandise"* of the saints are the purveyors of "itching ears theology". Their target is the group of believers with shallow roots; the group most likely to fall for their deceit and "fall away" from the faith altogether in times of tribulation. The direct impact of the charlatans, the fleecing of individual sheep, is bad enough, but a worse problem is the impact they have had on the overall church. To use a Biblical analogy, the "leaven" they introduced and the mainline ministers failed to exorcise, has infected the whole loaf and sullied the reputation of the entire church; or as Paul put it, *by reason of whom the way of truth shall be evil spoken of.* By not running them out of the ministry with the same zeal that Christ expelled the money changers, the church allowed their "itching ears theology" to infect, to some degree, every member and every church. When charlatans are allowed to operate with impunity within the church, the church can't blame outsiders for tarring us all with the same brush.

The last group within the church is made up of the saints or "the elect". Going back to the Parable Of The Sower, these are represented by the seed that fell on good ground (Mt 13:23). They are so deeply rooted that no amount of tribulation can stop them from bearing fruit. Persecute them even unto death and fruit will be born from the witness thereof. This group may take encouragement from this book, but they are beyond needing the cultivation this book aspires to. In keeping with the farming analogy, mature crops typically are not cultivated. If properly cultivated in youth, they are so deeply rooted and established at maturity they can suppress the competition without assistance. Their stature has grown to the point that there is no space between the rows; no place for the thorns to take root or compete for sunlight.

As you can see, it would be easy to get bogged down in the centuries old debate between the Calvinist and Arminian positions on eternal security. While there are many other verses I could cite, if the Calvinists are willing to dismiss all these, there is probably no reasonable limit to the number of verses they are willing to explain away. We're not going to settle that issue here. Pathological "belief persistence" is not easily overcome. Neither is the *"strong delusion"* God promised to send those who *"received not the love of the truth"* (2nd Thess 2:7-10). The point I set out to make is that the significant acceptance the Calvinist position (once saved always saved) enjoys, is based more on its appeal than the merits of the argument. It provides a classic example of formulating doctrine with an eye toward "tickling ears". Generally speaking, the Calvinist themselves have doubts about the basis for the doctrine of "once saved always saved". I feel safe in saying this because most will shun debate, pretend the doctrine is settled, attempt to diminish the opposing position, and engage in circular reasoning. These are all classic signs that a person knows he cannot defend a position on the merits.

I would hasten to add that, standing alone, this is not a salvation issue. There will be both Calvinist and Arminians in heaven. Having said that, I believe those who dogmatically promote either position out of impure motives will be called to account. That brings me to the question of why the church in later centuries chose to dogmatically teach the Calvinist position in light of so many passages in support of the much older Arminian position. I believe that question can be answered in one word; appeal. The Calvinist position helps people tamp down their insecurities, and hang on to their peace of mind. This can be a terrible thing. People who are insecure about their salvation may have good reason. Their insecurities need to be examined, not tamped down. They may be hanging on to a false sense of security based on the doctrines of men, or perhaps the *"doctrines of devils"*. On at least one occasion Paul admonished his people to *"examine yourselves, whether ye be in the faith"*. Obviously, this comment wasn't aimed at making them feel more secure! Paul understood that no sense of security is better than a false sense of security. A sense of security is false if it relies on anything other than our personal relationship with God and His promises. Doctrinal positions are of no consequence. I hold the Arminian position and my sense of security is not diminished. I know I cannot lose my salvation against my will. It cannot be taken from me or lost inadvertently. Just as I had to make a conscious decision to surrender to the Lord's will in order to be saved; I'd have to make a conscious decision to turn my back on Him and His plan for my life to be in danger of losing my salvation.

I believe the doctrine of "eternal security" is a relatively recent designer doctrine intended to broaden the gospels appeal; making it easier to keep the pews and coffers filled. Even if this was a minor factor in formulating the doctrine, and not the driving force, I'd still find it repulsive. Doctrine should be based exclusively on scripture, without bias or influence. If we embark on a study with a bias toward a desired outcome, our results are likely to be tainted by that desire. Far too many people begin their "study" with their minds made up. They aren't looking for facts to follow wherever they lead; they're looking to justify the conclusions they've already drawn.

As a group, the church has allowed appeal to not only become a factor in formulating doctrine, they've allowed it to become the driving force behind determining which doctrines to promote. The result is "itching ears theology" and a group of listeners that have been *"turned unto fables"*.

The charlatans and hucksters filling the airwaves with the *"doctrines of devils"* in a brazen attempt to separate the faithful from their money are at the extremes, but the mainline denominations are heading in the same direction, just at a slower pace and with a little more discretion. No one within the church is publicly calling the charlatans to account or standing up for the hard truths. This is strikingly similar to what is going on in the world of politics.

I'm aware of the pitfalls of mixing religion and politics but, it is so analogous, I can't resist drawing a political parallel. It has often been said that "Republicans want what the Democrats want; they just want it at a slower pace and at less cost." Progressive Democratic policies are spending the United States into financial collapse. Neoconservative Republican policies simply propose slowing the pace at which we spend ourselves into insolvency. Very few are proposing a fundamentally different direction whereby we spend within our means, beginning now.

To insure our peace of mind and support, progressive politicians tell us we can have cradle to grave entitlements without handing over the fruits of our labor or compromising our liberty. To insure our peace of mind and our donations, the charlatans in religion lead us to believe we can have salvation without surrender that leads to eternal life without commitment. They both sound like pretty sweet gigs if you can get 'em. The charlatans and hucksters, like the politicians who push progressive policies, are way out in front brazenly promoting their itching ears theology, while the more conservative ministers, like the so-called conservatives in our political system, are trying to show some restraint in terms of speed; but they nevertheless continue to move in the direction of telling people what they want to hear. It's another step in the direction of itching ears theology and another step toward financial collapse for the country. No one has the courage to promote the hard truths without which both the political and religious systems will fail. So, on to Armageddon we march. This should come as no surprise. The Bible tells us both systems will break down before Christ returns to establish His reign. If we wish to be part of the solution as opposed to part of the problem, we need to understand the implications of the fact that in the political world the government has nothing to give except that which it has taken and therefore all government largess comes at the expense of freedom. In the religious world, if we are to stand against the wiles of the Devil, we should be exhorted to *continue in the faith, and* made to understand *that we must through much tribulation enter into the kingdom of God.*

If Calvinist were to admit just the slightest possibility that the Arminians could be right, which they surely must, then the only basis for teaching the Calvinist position to the exclusion or diminution of the Arminian position is the desire to tickle ears.

Again, I'm not suggesting this or any other itching ears doctrine, considered alone, is the "smoking gun" proof for watered down theology or the conspiracy believed to be its underpinning. I am suggesting it is more circumstantial evidence that, when reviewed in total, will lead a spiritually enlightened person to conclude that a conspiracy is indeed afoot to dilute the church's doctrines in a way that will make it more difficult for the saints to stand against the deception that will be at the heart of the final spiritual battle. Attacks on doctrine are the Devil's artillery, intended to soften us before the all-out assault on truth. Make no mistake; from Adam and Eve to Armageddon, the battle has always been, and always will be, truth versus deception. But truth isn't just the objective; it is also the means, our sword and our shield. Any compromise whatsoever disarms us, undermining the objective, destroying morale, and weakening us both offensively and defensively. Compromising truth on any level in spiritual warfare is like questioning the rationale for taking the hill while putting down your rifle and stripping off your flak jacket. It's not a recipe for victory.

I should point out that not all Protestant denominations subscribe to the doctrine of eternal security. In fact, not all Baptist (the largest subgroup of Protestants) subscribe to the doctrine of eternal security. There is a very small sub-sect of Baptists, known as "Free Will Baptist", who hold the Arminian position that we retain our free will and thus the right to depart from the faith, even after we are saved. The Pentecostal denomination that I grew up in also holds the Arminian position. I'm sure there are others, but we are dwarfed in number by the main line Baptist and other Calvinist.

Chapter Four

"Prosperity Theology"

"Prosperity Theology", as taught by most of its purveyors, is nothing more than a run of the mill con game. The televangelists who promote it are the con artist. Gullible, and perhaps greedy, listeners are the "mark" (target). The idea that the Lord wants all His faithful to be healthy, wealthy, and wise is the "pitch". Suggesting that if you haven't gotten there yet it's only because you haven't been faithful enough; and that defect might be cured if you simply give more faithfully to the purveyor's ministry is the "hook". Of course, sending them money is the "sting". Like any truly successful con, the mark doesn't even know he's been had, and is likely to continue sending money.

In many cases the purveyors use the parable of the hundred fold increase talked about in Matthew 19:29 and Mark 10:29-30 to convince people they should place no limits on their generosity toward the purveyor's ministry because the Lord is going to pay them back one hundred times over. Regardless of how one interprets the parable of the hundredfold increase, any gift that is motivated by an attempt to manipulate God into making us rich, is almost guaranteed to have the opposite effect. But the con artist doesn't really care if the "marks" intentions are laudable or damnable, as long as they send a check.

Prosperity theology isn't always so brazen. Some of its forms are subtle. Purveyors may not always assert a direct cause and effect relationship between contributing to their ministry and receiving God's blessing. The more subtle purveyors are simply tickling ears to build audience, which in turn increases revenue. Subtle or direct, they are all based on the idea that what we want is what we need and we can manipulate God into giving it to us. We are wrong on both counts. We don't know what's best for us and God cannot be manipulated. We like to think that we know what's best for us, but I can prove that we don't. There is an old proverb that goes something like this:

> In Medieval times horses were used for both transportation and raising the family's crops. They were essential for survival. It was customary in those days that when a man came of age and fell in love, he'd take one of the family horses and set out to make his own way in the world. Against that backdrop, we have a very poor family with a young son that has come of age and fallen in love with a beautiful maiden. But the family has only one horse and is barely putting food on the table. Naturally, they go to bed every night praying that nothing will happen to that horse. Alas, they wake up one morning and their only horse is gone. This would seem like very bad news. But in a few days, the horse returns along with about a half dozen wild mares. This seems like very good news. The task of breaking the wild horses naturally falls to the young man of the family, and they all pray for his safety. In spite of the prayers, the young son is thrown by one of the horses and breaks his leg. This seems like very bad news, but a day or so later the king's army comes by conscripting every able bodied young man in the kingdom to go off to this battle where they are destined to be wiped out. Of course the broken leg keeps the young man from having to go. The story ends there. The moral of the story is, that without God's ability to see into the future, we can't possibility know what's best for us. Things

that seem good can turn out bad, and things that seem bad can turn out good. Unpredictable future events have to unfold before we can know whether a present event is good or bad.

While the setting for modern life is entirely different, the lessons are the same. God cannot be manipulated; and without His divine foresight, we can't possibly know what's best for us in a given situation. This shouldn't keep us from struggling toward our goals, but it should motivate us to seek knowledge of His will and keep us humble enough to bend to it when it is revealed. That brings to mind another illustration by another unknown author believed to be a battle weary Confederate soldier.

> I asked God for strength that I might achieve.
> I was made weak, that I might learn humbly to obey.
>
> I asked for health, that I might do greater things.
> I was given infirmity that I might do better things.
>
> I asked for riches, that I might be happy.
> I was given poverty, that I might be wise.
>
> I asked for power, that I might have the praise of men.
> I was given weakness, that I might feel the need of God.
>
> I asked for all things, that I might enjoy life.
> I was given life, that I might enjoy all things.
>
> I got nothing that I asked for - but everything I had hoped for.
>
> Almost despite myself, my unspoken prayers were answered.
>
> I am, among all men, most richly blessed.

There are so many profound lessons in the above illustration; it's hard to know where to begin. A slogan popular in AA circles is "There Is A God; and I'm Not It". The soldier in the above illustration had come to realize there were forces much greater than mere mortals controlling the events that steer our lives. He had seen that those forces were kind and gracious enough to bless him in spite of his own misguided efforts. He had come to grips with "There Is A God; And I'm Not It". In that moment he had found the humility that is a prerequisite to surrender and ultimate salvation. It started with the realization that he didn't know what was best for him and ended with reaching a level of spiritual maturity that enabled him to put aside what he thought he might want or need and ask only for knowledge of God's will for him and the strength to carry that out. He had come to trust that God would work all things together for the good of those that love Him (Romans 8:28).

"Prosperity Theology" on the other hand is not driven by humility. The "name it, and claim it" crowd puts forth the notion that anything we lay claim to in faith, God will provide. This position implies that we do know what's best and God can be manipulated into carrying out our wishes. It places us on the throne and relegates God to the position of celestial genie. If you're facing a mountain of debt, God will move it for you. If the cross you have to bear is sickness, God will relieve that burden if only you would, in faith, lay claim to excellent health. The name it and claim it crowd would suggest that all of God's potential blessings are available to every believer with the desire and faith to claim them. What about Paul's *thorn in the flesh* (2nd Cor 12:7)? Would the prosperity theologian suggest the writer of half of all the New Testament lacked the faith to heal himself? What about Timothy's stomach and his *often infirmities* (1st Tim 5:23). Then there was Trophimus who had to be left behind on one of Paul's missionary trips because he was *sick* (2nd Tim 4:20). Why didn't they "name it and claim it"? The answer is, God never promised to deliver us from all of life's travails; He only promised to be with us through them. It is through trials that we grow. Can we even imagine what a person without the benefit of trials or tribulations would be like; a person who had never been told "no"? I venture to say that person would be a monster. We grow in character and in spirit from our trials.

Then there are the televangelists who are really just motivational speakers who preach the power of positive thinking. This is just a lighter version of the "name it and claim it" doctrine. The power of positive thinking can indeed greatly improve one's lot in life and there is some Biblical teaching on the subject; but it is more a philosophy than it is a theology. Positive thinking will make us happier and put us in a frame of mind that is more conducive to success, but it cannot be used to turn God into our own private genie or celestial Santa Claus. When we get saved, God does not step down from the throne and hand it over to us. I know you've heard prayers that amounted to little more than a "to do" list for God. I've heard some that were literally jaw dropping. I'm sure these people would recoil from the notion, but they are effectively attempting to assume the throne and turn God into their administrative assistant. "I'll call the shots, you just make it happen."

A few charismatic motivational speakers have been able to wrap the power of positive thinking in the gospel so effectively they have been able to build huge followings. It's all a numbers game. Whether you refer to them as followers, believers, viewers, audiences, market share, contributors, or marks, the more of them you have, the more money you will raise. Unfortunately, that is the end that justifies the means for many of these "ministries".

To be clear, I want to point out that very few churches are preaching the most brazen forms of prosperity theology. Most are not preaching any form of it. But the churches that are constitute some of the largest, and very few, if any, remain completely unaffected by it. By way of the media, the more subtle forms of prosperity theology have crept into at least the pews, if not the pulpits, of even the most conservative churches. You see more and more churches today with their signs, billboards, marquees, newspaper ads, websites, and facebook pages, touting their programs and offerings. These are subtle indicators that the church is caught up in the process of competing for "contributors". They may not be as brazen as the charlatans; they may even be well intentioned, but they are moving in the direction of an industrialized and commercialized gospel.

I have nothing but sorrow and contempt for the purveyors of the more brazen forms of prosperity theology. While it may be true that many of their targets are victimized as much by their own greed as they are by the deception of the con artist; it is also true that many of the genuinely faithful are fleeced by these wolves in sheep's clothing. I believe there will be a special place in Hell for the purveyors who con saints that are barely getting by into sending money they can't spare; so the "ministry" can use that money to support an opulent life style.

Having said all that, my larger concern once again is the impact prosperity theology has on the overall body of believers we call the church. We are being softened up for the final assault. If we are continually taught that we have a right to expect to be healthy, wealthy, and wise, how will we ever stand the persecution and tribulation the Bible promised us in so many passages? A soldier charges the hill in the face of enemy fire because he has been trained to do so. His training has been brutally inclusive of even this worst case scenario. No one painted a pretty picture of combat. He is hoping for the best, but he is prepared for the worst. But most important, is the fact that as part of that training, he has purposed in his heart, well in advance, that when the order comes, he will obey rather than desert. This steely resolve is what makes a real soldier and it is something itching ears theology can never produce.

The modern church pays lip service to spiritual warfare and recruiting for the Lord's army, but "itching ears theology" will never produce anything but a sense of entitlement, and when the first casualties are taken in the spiritual battle to come, there will be a complete breakdown in morale, a complete and justifiable loss of respect for the chain of command, utter confusion, chaos, and mass desertion. If this sounds a lot like some of the scenes from the Book of Revelation, it probably isn't coincidence.

There is nothing being taught by the church today that would build the kind of steely resolve required to stand against the Antichrist during the Great Tribulation. The concepts of "salvation without surrender" (easybelieveism), "security without commitment" (eternal security), or "name it and claim it" (prosperity theology) certainly will not build resolve.

This is where I'm sure some of you are saying, what's the big deal, the saints aren't going to be here for the Great Tribulation anyway, they'll all be "raptured". That brings us to the chapter on "escapeism".

Chapter Five

"Escapeism"

So far we have talked about the church teaching "salvation without surrender", "security without commitment", and "prosperity without effort". For the church leader looking to build and maintain a happy, loyal, and generous following, that leaves the prospect of persecution and/or tribulation as the only obstacle to bringing more people into the church. Although the Bible tells us to expect scorn from the world and church history is replete with examples of persecution and tribulation, the modern televangelist, and ultimately the church, decided that emphasizing this part of the Christian walk was not conducive to building a large, enthusiastic, and generous following. They needed an interpretation of scripture that minimized or eliminated hardship and suffering. This led to the early twentieth century doctrine of an imminent pre-tribulation "rapture" of the church. With this piece of doctrine in place the church could add "deliverance without hardship" to "salvation without surrender", "security without commitment" and "prosperity without effort". What a deal! The Christian could now expect to be transported from hedonism to heaven on a feather bed!

I'm not going to make a big deal out of the fact that the word "rapture" doesn't appear in the Bible; at least not the one that has enjoyed the most widespread use over the past four hundred years (The King James Version). "Rapture" also did not appear in 8 of the other 10 translations I checked. In no translation did it appear in the context of the saints being "raptured". I won't make a big deal out of it, because even though the word doesn't appear, the concept of the earth being "harvested" is well documented. I don't object to people substituting the word "rapture" for "harvest". This isn't about word games; it's about the timing of the "harvest".

I am going to spend a lot of time on the idea of a pre-tribulation rapture ("escapeism") because, of all the "itching ears theology", it has the most questionable foundation and the most potential for destruction in terms of the church as a whole. In addition, its broad acceptance, combined with a complete lack of Biblical support, make it the most glaring example of truth being sacrificed in the interest of "appeal" and the clearest evidence of a sinister deceptive force at work. Finally, I would say that much time will be spent on the signs of the end because we are instructed by scripture to watch for them and therefore avoid being taken by surprise (Mt 24:42-51). No one will know the day or the hour; but we can all know the general time frame. We are also assured that our efforts to understand eschatology will be rewarded. That promise is found in Revelation 1:3; *"Blessed is he that readeth, and they that hear the words of this prophecy, and keep those things which are written therein: for the time is at hand"*. There will be no billboards or public service announcements telling us we are about to enter the "tribulation period". Nevertheless, the signs, however subtle, will be clear enough to the spiritually mature student of scripture. There will be more about that as we go through the Biblical texts that establish a timeline.

To lay the foundation for understanding eschatology, there are certain passages of scripture that we need to get our heads wrapped around before we can hope to build a solid systematic theology on the subject. To this end, I'm going to insert certain passages that I believe are essential to understanding the nature and timing of the *"harvest of the earth"*. The use of the phrase *"harvest of the earth"* is not accidental. It is lifted directly from scripture in the context of God gathering the saints unto Himself at the end of time. All other things being equal, I prefer using words and phrases lifted directly from scripture.

Reading the following passages of scripture will make it easier to comprehend the details we'll fill in later.

Daniel 8:11(KJV)
[11]Yea, he magnified himself even to the prince of the host, and by him the daily sacrifice was taken away, and the place of his sanctuary was cast down.

This is an obvious reference to the Antichrist. Although there might be several people in history that could loosely fit this description, I believe the ultimate reference is to "the" final Antichrist that will reign during the tribulation period and lead the world to Armageddon.

Daniel 8:23-26(KJV)
[23]And in the latter time of their kingdom, when the transgressors are come to the full, a king of fierce countenance, and understanding dark sentences, shall stand up.
[24]And his power shall be mighty, but not by his own power: and he shall destroy wonderfully, and shall prosper, and practice, and shall destroy the mighty and the holy people.
[25]And through his policy also he shall cause craft to prosper in his hand; and he shall magnify himself in his heart, and by peace shall destroy many: he shall also stand up against the Prince of princes; but he shall be broken without hand.
[26]And the vision of the evening and the morning which was told is true: wherefore shut thou up the vision; for it shall be for many days.

The phrases used in this passage are intriguing. Consider the meaning of "understanding dark sentences", "destroy wonderfully", "cause craft to prosper", and "by peace shall destroy many". I take "understanding dark sentences" to mean that this person's skill in the art of subterfuge will be unparalleled in human history. His deceptions will be so cleverly devised that people will have no idea they are being duped. I believe "destroy wonderfully" speaks to both the efficiency with which he destroys, as well as the fact that he manages to do it in such a way that others receive the blame. It could already be said that we live in a world that rewards the crafty. Those who are able to "spin" facts in a way that gives them credit for all things good while deflecting blame for all things bad, will indeed "cause craft to prosper". "By peace shall destroy many" is suggestive of the extent to which he will have duped his followers. I fully expect he will be suggesting to his followers that he is on a quest for peace even as he leads them toward Armageddon. Subterfuge is the use of subtle deceptions in order to advance a cleverly devised strategy; usually aimed at gaining an advantage or control over others. We must not underestimate the power of subterfuge employed by stunningly clever and strategically subtle dark forces.

Daniel 9:27(KJV)

27 And he shall confirm the covenant with many for one week: and in the midst of the week he shall cause the sacrifice and the oblation to cease, and for the overspreading of abominations he shall make it desolate, even until the consummation, and that determined shall be poured upon the desolate.

Most Bible scholars interpret "week" in this context to be a "week" of seven years, and the seven years to be the tribulation period. There is ample support for this theory. Thus, many believe the desecration of the temple and the end of sacrifices will come in the middle of the 7 year tribulation period. I would caution against putting too much stock in this interpretation; not because it's likely to be wrong, but because even if it's true it might not help in terms of trying to determine the day or the hour. To begin with, there will be no marker indicating exactly when to hit the stopwatch and start counting off the 7 years. In addition, there is presently no temple to desecrate or sacrifices to halt; at least not in the Old Testament sense. Perhaps the temple will be rebuilt and sacrifices resumed; or perhaps some of this is figurative and we need to look deeper. In any case, the beginning of the timeline is not precise and neither are the milestones. We need to continue to watch for corroborating signs and pray for discernment.

Daniel 11:23-24(KJV)
23And after the league made with him he shall work deceitfully: for he shall come up, and shall become strong with a small people.
24He shall enter peaceably even upon the fattest places of the province; and he shall do that which his fathers have not done, nor his fathers' fathers; he shall scatter among them the prey, and spoil, and riches: yea, and he shall forecast his devices against the strong holds, even for a time.

No surprise of course that he *"shall work deceitfully"*. He will start with a relatively small following. His will be a mission of *"peace"*. As he begins to gain power, he will build on that momentum by sharing the spoils of his victories. Far too many people are going to be looking for the personification of the Devil, but he will be well disguised as *"an angel of light"*.

Daniel 11:30-37(KJV)
30For the ships of Chittim shall come against him: therefore he shall be grieved, and return, and have indignation against the holy covenant: so shall he do; he shall even return, and have intelligence with them that forsake the holy covenant.
31And arms shall stand on his part, and they shall pollute the sanctuary of strength, and shall take away the daily sacrifice, and they shall place the abomination that maketh desolate.
32And such as do wickedly against the covenant shall he corrupt by flatteries: but the people that do know their God shall be strong, and do exploits.
33And they that understand among the people shall instruct many: yet they shall fall by the sword, and by flame, by captivity, and by spoil, many days.
34Now when they shall fall, they shall be holpen with a little help: but many shall cleave to them with flatteries.
35And some of them of understanding shall fall, to try them, and to purge, and to make them white, even to the time of the end: because it is yet for a time appointed.

^{36}And the king shall do according to his will; and he shall exalt himself, and magnify himself above every god, and shall speak marvellous things against the God of gods, and shall prosper till the indignation be accomplished: for that that is determined shall be done.
^{37}Neither shall he regard the God of his fathers, nor the desire of women, nor regard any god: for he shall magnify himself above all.

Apparently he will suffer a setback that will cause him to turn on the children of God more openly. This is when the real carnage begins. Many, including *"they that understand"* and *"instruct many"*, will fall victim to the Antichrist. This is to *"try them, and to purge, and to make them white"*. It has been this way throughout history. No one is exempt from the fact *"that we must through much tribulation enter into the kingdom of God"* (Acts 14:22).

Daniel 12:1-4(KJV)
^{1}And at that time shall Michael stand up, the great prince which standeth for the children of thy people: and there shall be a time of trouble, such as never was since there was a nation even to that same time: and at that time thy people shall be delivered, every one that shall be found written in the book.
^{2}And many of them that sleep in the dust of the earth shall awake, some to everlasting life, and some to shame and everlasting contempt.
^{3}And they that be wise shall shine as the brightness of the firmament; and they that turn many to righteousness as the stars for ever and ever.
^{4}But thou, O Daniel, shut up the words, and seal the book, even to the time of the end: many shall run to and fro, and knowledge shall be increased.

This is an obvious reference to the *"harvest of the earth"* that takes place in Revelation 14. Beyond the mid-point of the tribulation period, after the Antichrist has revealed himself to anyone with any Bible knowledge by desecrating the temple and declaring war on the saints, the situation will go from bad to worse; from tribulation to "Great Tribulation". The covert war will devolve into open conflict and what Daniel describes as "a time of trouble, such as never was since there was a nation…". In Matthew 24:21-22, Jesus describes this time; *²¹For then shall be great tribulation, such as was not since the beginning of the world to this time, no, nor ever shall be. ²²And except those days should be shortened, there should no flesh be saved: but for the elect's sake those days shall be shortened.* Those days of Great Tribulation are shortened when Jesus and His angels return for the saints.

Daniel 12:8-13(KJV)

⁸And I heard, but I understood not: then said I, O my Lord, what shall be the end of these things?

⁹And he said, Go thy way, Daniel: for the words are closed up and sealed till the time of the end.

¹⁰Many shall be purified, and made white, and tried; but the wicked shall do wickedly: and none of the wicked shall understand; but the wise shall understand.

¹¹And from the time that the daily sacrifice shall be taken away, and the abomination that maketh desolate set up, there shall be a thousand two hundred and ninety days.

¹²Blessed is he that waiteth, and cometh to the thousand three hundred and five and thirty days.

¹³But go thou thy way till the end be: for thou shalt rest, and stand in thy lot at the end of the days.

Again, I wouldn't suggest that anyone has a lock on interpreting this passage. We can't be sure how much is literal and how much is figurative. Apart from the math, I don't think anyone fully understands the difference between the 1290 days and the 1335 days.

I should also point out that some "scholars" maintain that the whole book of Daniel is history, not prophecy. Those who are quick to adopt any position that will cast doubt on the authenticity of scripture will tell you the Book of Daniel was written hundreds of years after Daniel was dead and years after Antiochus Epiphanes did many of the things described in the book attributed to Daniel. They contend it was written as an autobiographical prophecy; but in reality it is a history written in the first person autobiographical form hundreds of years after the fact. This is a sophisticate's way of saying it is a fraud. Most conservative scholars would disagree on both counts. I'm operating on the assumption that Daniel the Prophet wrote the Book of Daniel about 400 years before Antiochus Epiphanes persecuted and slaughtered tens of thousands of Jews and desecrated the temple in 167 BC.

In Matthew 24:15, two hundred years after Antiochus Epiphanes, Christ pointed to the prophecies of Daniel in warning of a still future event. Was Christ hoodwinked? Was He ignorant in terms of the reign of Antiochus? Of course, the same folks who would suggest the prophecies of Daniel were written after the facts they describe, would tell you that Matthew was written after the events it pretends to foretell. They would suggest that Matthew was written after 70AD and portrayed Christ as prophesying about the Roman sacking of the temple in 70AD and the persecution of the saints under the Roman emperor Nero. I'm not going to get sucked into a debate over when specific books of the Bible were written. Since exact dates are impossible to pin down, that's an academic discussion that will go on perhaps indefinitely. I might concede that Matthew was written after 70AD, but I do not believe it purported to prophesy about events known to be in the past except to the extent that it knew those events were destined to be repeated. I'm not willing to accept that major books of the Bible are, in any way, frauds.

Since they didn't have copiers, computers, flash drives, microfilm or any other modern method of preserving manuscripts, they preserved them the only way they could, by replication. Professionals, known as scribes, dedicated their lives to the process. They literally rewrote manuscripts, letter by letter. We are not likely to ever know the precise date of the original manuscript or the point at which deterioration compelled a scribe to produce the first copy. We cannot know where the oldest manuscripts in our possession fit into the chain of manuscripts that were transcribed over the centuries. Assuming the oldest manuscript you can find is the original and dating it accordingly invites the kind of error that has led some to suggest a later writing for Daniel.

Debates over who was speaking, to whom they were speaking, and the date of the writing are just a few of the ways one can get bogged down while trying to wrest the meaning from scripture by pure intellect. If you're not being spiritually led to an interpretation, you're probably being misled. You may recall in the chapter on "easybelieveism" we quoted from 1ˢᵗ Cor 2:14 *...the natural man receiveth not the things of the Spirit of God: for they are foolishness unto him: neither can he know them, because they are spiritually discerned.* The spiritual truths of the Bible are cloaked in metaphors, allegories, types, foreshadowings, and parables. One has to have the right spiritual mindset to penetrate the veils. Biblical interpretation is a very intellectual exercise, but it's not mechanical intellect; it's intuitive or spiritual intellect. It's not compiling data, it's discerning.

I take the position that all references to the Antichrist, the end of days, the desecration of the temple, the tribulation period, etc. are references to future events. This does not preclude them from applying to historical events as well. The Bible and history are literally full of events that are foreshadowings of events to come. History really does repeat itself. Or as the writer of Ecclesiastes 1:9-10 says, *The thing that hath been, it is that which shall be; and that which is done is that which shall be done: and there is no new thing under the sun. ¹⁰Is there any thing whereof it may be said, See, this is new? it hath been already of old time, which was before us.* I see the references in Daniel as applying to both the Antiochus of 167 BC and the future Antichrist. Antiochus may have been a foreshadowing of the Antichrist in much the same way that Joseph of the Old Testament is considered a foreshadowing of Christ. Joseph was rejected by his own; dead as far as his father was concerned; yet he figuratively came back to life and went on to save the known world from mass starvation.

As an aside, I would note that those who look at these prophecies as pointing to future events are appropriately called Futurist. Those who subscribe to the view that these events are all in the past are called Preterist. This book is written from the Futurist point of view because it is the view I hold and share with the overwhelming majority of all other Protestants.

Now let us move on to the Parable Of The Wheats And The Tares:

Matthew 13:24-30(KJV)
[24]*Another parable put he forth unto them, saying, The kingdom of heaven is likened unto a man which sowed good seed in his field:*
[25]*But while men slept, his enemy came and sowed tares among the wheat, and went his way.*
[26]*But when the blade was sprung up, and brought forth fruit, then appeared the tares also.*
[27]*So the servants of the householder came and said unto him, Sir, didst not thou sow good seed in thy field? from whence then hath it tares?*
[28]*He said unto them, An enemy hath done this. The servants said unto him, Wilt thou then that we go and gather them up?*
[29]*But he said, Nay; lest while ye gather up the tares, ye root up also the wheat with them.*
[30]*Let both grow together until the harvest: and in the time of harvest I will say to the reapers, Gather ye together first the tares, and bind them in bundles to burn them: but gather the wheat into my barn.*

Matthew 13:36-43(KJV)
[36]*Then Jesus sent the multitude away, and went into the house: and his disciples came unto him, saying, Declare unto us the parable of the tares of the field.*
[37]*He answered and said unto them, He that soweth the good seed is the Son of man;*
[38]*The field is the world; the good seed are the children of the kingdom; but the tares are the children of the wicked one;*
[39]*The enemy that sowed them is the devil; the harvest is the end of the world; and the reapers are the angels.*
[40]*As therefore the tares are gathered and burned in the fire; so shall it be in the end of this world.*
[41]*The Son of man shall send forth his angels, and they shall gather out of his kingdom all things that offend, and them which do iniquity;*
[42]*And shall cast them into a furnace of fire: there shall be wailing and gnashing of teeth.*
[43]*Then shall the righteous shine forth as the sun in the kingdom of their Father. Who hath ears to hear, let him hear.*

The Parable Of The Wheats And The Tares provides a broad outline of the entire span of human history and reveals God's attitude about the coexistence of good and evil. It is also instructive in terms of the "harvest" sequence and the players involved. Notice how the role of angels in the "harvest" synchronizes with Matthew 24:31 and Revelation 14:15-19.

While The Parable Of The Wheats And The Tares in Matthew 13 succinctly summarizes the divine perspective on all of human history, The Olivet Discourse in Matthew 24 zeros in on events leading up to and including the "harvest". Because the words are from Christ Himself and spoken in direct response to a specific question about the second coming, I believe The Olivet Discourse (Matthew 24) is the most instructive Biblical text on the subject of eschatology.

Matthew 24:3-31(KJV)

³And as he sat upon the mount of Olives, the disciples came unto him privately, saying, Tell us, when shall these things be? and what shall be the sign of thy coming, and of the end of the world?
⁴And Jesus answered and said unto them, Take heed that no man deceive you.
⁵For many shall come in my name, saying, I am Christ; and shall deceive many.
⁶And ye shall hear of wars and rumours of wars: see that ye be not troubled: for all these things must come to pass, but the end is not yet.
⁷For nation shall rise against nation, and kingdom against kingdom: and there shall be famines, and pestilences, and earthquakes, in divers places.
⁸All these are the beginning of sorrows.
⁹Then shall they deliver you up to be afflicted, and shall kill you: and ye shall be hated of all nations for my name's sake.
¹⁰And then shall many be offended, and shall betray one another, and shall hate one another.
¹¹And many false prophets shall rise, and shall deceive many.
¹²And because iniquity shall abound, the love of many shall wax cold.
¹³But he that shall endure unto the end, the same shall be saved.

¹⁴And this gospel of the kingdom shall be preached in all the world for a witness unto all nations; and then shall the end come.

¹⁵When ye therefore shall see the abomination of desolation, spoken of by Daniel the prophet, stand in the holy place, (whoso readeth, let him understand:)

¹⁶Then let them which be in Judaea flee into the mountains:

¹⁷Let him which is on the housetop not come down to take any thing out of his house:

¹⁸Neither let him which is in the field return back to take his clothes.

¹⁹And woe unto them that are with child, and to them that give suck in those days!

²⁰But pray ye that your flight be not in the winter, neither on the sabbath day:

²¹For then shall be great tribulation, such as was not since the beginning of the world to this time, no, nor ever shall be.

²²And except those days should be shortened, there should no flesh be saved: but for the elect's sake those days shall be shortened.

²³Then if any man shall say unto you, Lo, here is Christ, or there; believe it not.

²⁴For there shall arise false Christs, and false prophets, and shall show great signs and wonders; insomuch that, if it were possible, they shall deceive the very elect.

²⁵Behold, I have told you before.

²⁶Wherefore if they shall say unto you, Behold, he is in the desert; go not forth: behold, he is in the secret chambers; believe it not.

²⁷For as the lightning cometh out of the east, and shineth even unto the west; so shall also the coming of the Son of man be.

²⁸For wheresoever the carcase is, there will the eagles be gathered together.

²⁹Immediately after the tribulation of those days shall the sun be darkened, and the moon shall not give her light, and the stars shall fall from heaven, and the powers of the heavens shall be shaken:

³⁰And then shall appear the sign of the Son of man in heaven: and then shall all the tribes of the earth mourn, and they shall see the Son of man coming in the clouds of heaven with power and great glory.

³¹And he shall send his angels with a great sound of a trumpet, and they shall gather together his elect from the four winds, from one end of heaven to the other.

In the interest of hiding the exact date, while simultaneously providing the saints all the clues they need to stay ahead of events as they unfold, He told us what to look for as the time approaches. I believe the key phrase is "stay ahead of events as they unfold". This is the ultimate "need to know basis". Without giving anyone specific advance notice, the spiritually connected saints who constantly search the scriptures will know what they need to know, when they need to know it. All others will remain in the dark. In these brief pages I cannot offer a detailed verse by verse commentary on Matthew 24. Significant portions of it will be discussed at more length later in this chapter, but I also encourage you to read it over and over, parsing every word. For example; the exact timing might not be revealed, but in verse 29, we learn that the second coming will be *"after the tribulation of those days"*. This language is not ambiguous; after means after. Any doctrine that places the "harvest" (rapture) before the tribulation period has to explain away everything that Christ told us about His return.

1 Corinthians 15:50-55(KJV)

[50]Now this I say, brethren, that flesh and blood cannot inherit the kingdom of God; neither doth corruption inherit incorruption.
[51]Behold, I show you a mystery; We shall not all sleep, but we shall all be changed,
[52]In a moment, in the twinkling of an eye, at the last trump: for the trumpet shall sound, and the dead shall be raised incorruptible, and we shall be changed.
[53]For this corruptible must put on incorruption, and this mortal must put on immortality.
[54]So when this corruptible shall have put on incorruption, and this mortal shall have put on immortality, then shall be brought to pass the saying that is written, Death is swallowed up in victory.
[55]O death, where is thy sting? O grave, where is thy victory?

There are several passages of scripture that associate a trumpet with the second coming of Christ and the *"harvest of the earth"*, but this is the only passage that is specific as to the particular trumpet. First Corinthians 15:52, tells us the second coming will be preceded by "the last trump". This is great! All we have to do is find the scripture where the sounding of the "last trump" is recorded. Naturally, it will be in the book of Revelation, where end time events are laid out in considerable detail. Some of you will recall the seven seals of Revelation that are opened in Chapters 5 through 8. You may also recall that the seventh seal contains within it seven trumpets. These in turn are sounded in chapters 8 through 11. The one and only "last trump" is sounded in Rev 11:15. In accordance with timelines laid out by Daniel, Christ, and Paul, the "harvest" is depicted in the chapters that follow Revelation 11:15; most specifically in Revelation 14. Obviously, the timing is not pre-tribulation. I want to be kind, but I just don't see how either scholarship or discernment can lead one to a pre-tribulation rapture position.

1 Thessalonians 4:13-17(KJV)

13But I would not have you to be ignorant, brethren, concerning them which are asleep, that ye sorrow not, even as others which have no hope.
14For if we believe that Jesus died and rose again, even so them also which sleep in Jesus will God bring with him.
15For this we say unto you by the word of the Lord, that we which are alive and remain unto the coming of the Lord shall not prevent them which are asleep.
16For the Lord himself shall descend from heaven with a shout, with the voice of the archangel, and with the trump of God: and the dead in Christ shall rise first:
17Then we which are alive and remain shall be caught up together with them in the clouds, to meet the Lord in the air: and so shall we ever be with the Lord.

First Thessalonians 4:13-17 associates both a trumpet and clouds with the second coming and "harvest". These themes are consistent throughout scripture. Paul's intent may have been to reassure the saints in Thessalonica that, whether dead or alive, they need not worry about missing the second coming and harvest. But in so doing, he also reinforces the timeline and sequence of events surrounding the "harvest". Paul expands on this theme in his second letter to the Thessalonians. Note that all these passages are specific teachings on the specific subject of eschatology. We cannot be accused of pulling passages out of context to support our theology or timeline.

2 Thessalonians 2:1-12(KJV)

¹Now we beseech you, brethren, by the coming of our Lord Jesus Christ, and by our gathering together unto him,

²That ye be not soon shaken in mind, or be troubled, neither by spirit, nor by word, nor by letter as from us, as that the day of Christ is at hand.

³Let no man deceive you by any means: for that day shall not come, except there come a falling away first, and that man of sin be revealed, the son of perdition;

⁴Who opposeth and exalteth himself above all that is called God, or that is worshipped; so that he as God sitteth in the temple of God, showing himself that he is God.

⁵Remember ye not, that, when I was yet with you, I told you these things?

⁶And now ye know what withholdeth that he might be revealed in his time.

⁷For the mystery of iniquity doth already work: only he who now letteth will let, until he be taken out of the way.

⁸And then shall that Wicked be revealed, whom the Lord shall consume with the spirit of his mouth, and shall destroy with the brightness of his coming:

⁹Even him, whose coming is after the working of Satan with all power and signs and lying wonders,

¹⁰And with all deceivableness of unrighteousness in them that perish; because they received not the love of the truth, that they might be saved.

¹¹And for this cause God shall send them strong delusion, that they should believe a lie:

¹²That they all might be damned who believed not the truth, but had pleasure in unrighteousness.

This passage provides considerable detail. We are told that the second coming will be preceded by a "falling away" from the faith and the revealing of the Antichrist. We are also told that the weapon of choice of the Antichrist will be deception, and anyone who isn't a devoted lover of truth will be duped, deluded, and damned. It's powerful language.

With that understanding, let us examine Chapters 5 through 14 of the Book of Revelation.

Revelation 5:1-14(KJV)

¹And I saw in the right hand of him that sat on the throne a book written within and on the backside, sealed with seven seals.

²And I saw a strong angel proclaiming with a loud voice, Who is worthy to open the book, and to loose the seals thereof?

³And no man in heaven, nor in earth, neither under the earth, was able to open the book, neither to look thereon.

⁴And I wept much, because no man was found worthy to open and to read the book, neither to look thereon.

⁵And one of the elders saith unto me, Weep not: behold, the Lion of the tribe of Juda, the Root of David, hath prevailed to open the book, and to loose the seven seals thereof.

⁶And I beheld, and, lo, in the midst of the throne and of the four beasts, and in the midst of the elders, stood a Lamb as it had been slain, having seven horns and seven eyes, which are the seven Spirits of God sent forth into all the earth.

⁷And he came and took the book out of the right hand of him that sat upon the throne.

⁸And when he had taken the book, the four beasts and four and twenty elders fell down before the Lamb, having every one of them harps, and golden vials full of odours, which are the prayers of saints.

⁹And they sung a new song, saying, Thou art worthy to take the book, and to open the seals thereof: for thou wast slain, and hast redeemed us to God by thy blood out of every kindred, and tongue, and people, and nation;

¹⁰And hast made us unto our God kings and priests: and we shall reign on the earth.

¹¹And I beheld, and I heard the voice of many angels round about the throne and the beasts and the elders: and the number of them was ten thousand times ten thousand, and thousands of thousands;

¹²Saying with a loud voice, Worthy is the Lamb that was slain to receive power, and riches, and wisdom, and strength, and honour, and glory, and blessing.

¹³And every creature which is in heaven, and on the earth, and under the earth, and such as are in the sea, and all that are in them, heard I

saying, Blessing, and honour, and glory, and power, be unto him that sitteth upon the throne, and unto the Lamb for ever and ever.
14 And the four beasts said, Amen. And the four and twenty elders fell down and worshipped him that liveth for ever and ever.

This passage paints a word picture of a scroll sealed with seven seals. It contains God's plan for the end of time. No one, except Christ Himself was worthy to break the seals and reveal the plan. As the seals are released in future chapters, more of the plan is revealed. It is instructive that the seals are broken sequentially and methodically. It is the same way that eschatology will be revealed to the believer. We can have a general understanding of God's eschatological plan, but no one is going to be able to fully understand and predict exactly how events will unfold in advance. Many have tried and sacrificed their credibility in the process. If we follow world events while praying and studying the scriptures daily, what we need to know will be revealed to us as we need to know it. Those who are not rooted in the scripture will be banished into darkness, in more ways than one.

Revelation 6:1-17(KJV)
1 And I saw when the Lamb opened one of the seals, and I heard, as it were the noise of thunder, one of the four beasts saying, Come and see.
2 And I saw, and behold a white horse: and he that sat on him had a bow; and a crown was given unto him: and he went forth conquering, and to conquer.
3 And when he had opened the second seal, I heard the second beast say, Come and see.
4 And there went out another horse that was red: and power was given to him that sat thereon to take peace from the earth, and that they should kill one another: and there was given unto him a great sword.
5 And when he had opened the third seal, I heard the third beast say, Come and see. And I beheld, and lo a black horse; and he that sat on him had a pair of balances in his hand.
6 And I heard a voice in the midst of the four beasts say, A measure of wheat for a penny, and three measures of barley for a penny; and see thou hurt not the oil and the wine.

⁷And when he had opened the fourth seal, I heard the voice of the fourth beast say, Come and see.

⁸And I looked, and behold a pale horse: and his name that sat on him was Death, and Hell followed with him. And power was given unto them over the fourth part of the earth, to kill with sword, and with hunger, and with death, and with the beasts of the earth.

⁹And when he had opened the fifth seal, I saw under the altar the souls of them that were slain for the word of God, and for the testimony which they held:

¹⁰And they cried with a loud voice, saying, How long, O Lord, holy and true, dost thou not judge and avenge our blood on them that dwell on the earth?

¹¹And white robes were given unto every one of them; and it was said unto them, that they should rest yet for a little season, until their fellowservants also and their brethren, that should be killed as they were, should be fulfilled.

¹²And I beheld when he had opened the sixth seal, and, lo, there was a great earthquake; and the sun became black as sackcloth of hair, and the moon became as blood;

¹³And the stars of heaven fell unto the earth, even as a fig tree casteth her untimely figs, when she is shaken of a mighty wind.

¹⁴And the heaven departed as a scroll when it is rolled together; and every mountain and island were moved out of their places.

¹⁵And the kings of the earth, and the great men, and the rich men, and the chief captains, and the mighty men, and every bondman, and every free man, hid themselves in the dens and in the rocks of the mountains;

¹⁶And said to the mountains and rocks, Fall on us, and hide us from the face of him that sitteth on the throne, and from the wrath of the Lamb:

¹⁷For the great day of his wrath is come; and who shall be able to stand?

It is impossible to say how much of Revelation Chapter 6 is literal and how much is metaphorical. John the Revelator had no choice but to describe what he saw in the language of his day. Imagine trying to describe a nuclear holocaust without being able to use any modern words such as intercontinental ballistic missile, atomic blast, nuclear winter, etc. If he witnessed intercontinental ballistic missiles burning as they re-entered the earth's atmosphere and exploding on impact, he would have almost certainly described the scene as *"the stars of heaven fell unto the earth"* Whether it caused an earthquake or not, it would almost certainly feel like one. The craters and the rock and debris blown from them, would make it appear that the mountains and islands were being re-arranged. The dust, debris, and nuclear fallout would cause the sun to be darkened and nuclear winter to fall upon the earth. No doubt, even if they weren't suffering from radiation sickness, many would wish for death.

It is important to remember that we have no way of knowing the time lapse between Chapters 5 and 14. We can surmise from the text that some considerable time is involved, but I believe it is intentionally impossible to build a precise timeline. In Chapter 6, verse 11, the martyrs that are crying out for vengeance are told they must wait *"for a little season"*. This is a prime example of intentionally vague.

Although the people described in Revelation 6:16-17 conclude that the wrath of the Lamb is upon them, they are only partially right. God did indeed set the stage, and He is allowing the events to unfold, but the things being described up to this point are calamities that mankind is bringing upon himself. It is not coincidence that the word "wrath" does not appear again until Revelation 11:18, three verses after *"the last trump"*. Even then it is just a proclamation that the wrath of God is imminent. The actual wrath of God isn't poured out on the earth until Revelation Chapter 16; after the *"harvest of the earth"* takes place in Chapter 14. In Chapters 5 through 13 we see God's people having to deal with the consequences of the world they helped create, or allowed to come about; but, they are *"harvested"* before the actual wrath of God is poured out on the *"tares"*.

Revelation 7:1-17(KJV)
¹And after these things I saw four angels standing on the four corners of the earth, holding the four winds of the earth, that the wind should not blow on the earth, nor on the sea, nor on any tree.

2And I saw another angel ascending from the east, having the seal of the living God: and he cried with a loud voice to the four angels, to whom it was given to hurt the earth and the sea,

3Saying, Hurt not the earth, neither the sea, nor the trees, till we have sealed the servants of our God in their foreheads.

4And I heard the number of them which were sealed: and there were sealed an hundred and forty and four thousand of all the tribes of the children of Israel.

5Of the tribe of Judah were sealed twelve thousand. Of the tribe of Reuben were sealed twelve thousand. Of the tribe of Gad were sealed twelve thousand.

6Of the tribe of Aser were sealed twelve thousand. Of the tribe of Nepthalim were sealed twelve thousand. Of the tribe of Manasses were sealed twelve thousand.

7Of the tribe of Simeon were sealed twelve thousand. Of the tribe of Levi were sealed twelve thousand. Of the tribe of Issachar were sealed twelve thousand.

8Of the tribe of Zabulon were sealed twelve thousand. Of the tribe of Joseph were sealed twelve thousand. Of the tribe of Benjamin were sealed twelve thousand.

9After this I beheld, and, lo, a great multitude, which no man could number, of all nations, and kindreds, and people, and tongues, stood before the throne, and before the Lamb, clothed with white robes, and palms in their hands;

10And cried with a loud voice, saying, Salvation to our God which sitteth upon the throne, and unto the Lamb.

11And all the angels stood round about the throne, and about the elders and the four beasts, and fell before the throne on their faces, and worshipped God,

12Saying, Amen: Blessing, and glory, and wisdom, and thanksgiving, and honour, and power, and might, be unto our God for ever and ever. Amen.

13And one of the elders answered, saying unto me, What are these which are arrayed in white robes? and whence came they?

14And I said unto him, Sir, thou knowest. And he said to me, These are they which came out of great tribulation, and have washed their robes, and made them white in the blood of the Lamb.

[15]Therefore are they before the throne of God, and serve him day and night in his temple: and he that sitteth on the throne shall dwell among them.

[16]They shall hunger no more, neither thirst any more; neither shall the sun light on them, nor any heat.

[17]For the Lamb which is in the midst of the throne shall feed them, and shall lead them unto living fountains of waters: and God shall wipe away all tears from their eyes.

In Chapter 7 we see the sealing of the 144,000; 12,000 from each of the 12 tribes of Israel. It appears they are being singled out for divine protection from the calamities that remain. They are to become "*the firstfruits*" of "*the harvest of the earth*". We see them being presented as such in the first 4 verses of Revelation Chapter 14. We also see in Chapter 7 those who have overcome great tribulation by the blood of the Lamb. It's impossible to say if these saints were martyrs from all time, or casualties just from the calamities that began with the opening of the first six seals. The text says they came out of "great tribulation", but not necessarily out of THE great tribulation. Obviously, martyrs from any period have endured a great tribulation.

Revelation 8:1-13(KJV)

[1]And when he had opened the seventh seal, there was silence in heaven about the space of half an hour.

[2]And I saw the seven angels which stood before God; and to them were given seven trumpets.

[3]And another angel came and stood at the altar, having a golden censer; and there was given unto him much incense, that he should offer it with the prayers of all saints upon the golden altar which was before the throne.

[4]And the smoke of the incense, which came with the prayers of the saints, ascended up before God out of the angel's hand.

[5]And the angel took the censer, and filled it with fire of the altar, and cast it into the earth: and there were voices, and thunderings, and lightnings, and an earthquake.

[6]And the seven angels which had the seven trumpets prepared themselves to sound.

⁷The first angel sounded, and there followed hail and fire mingled with blood, and they were cast upon the earth: and the third part of trees was burnt up, and all green grass was burnt up.

⁸And the second angel sounded, and as it were a great mountain burning with fire was cast into the sea: and the third part of the sea became blood;

⁹And the third part of the creatures which were in the sea, and had life, died; and the third part of the ships were destroyed.

¹⁰And the third angel sounded, and there fell a great star from heaven, burning as it were a lamp, and it fell upon the third part of the rivers, and upon the fountains of waters;

¹¹And the name of the star is called Wormwood: and the third part of the waters became wormwood; and many men died of the waters, because they were made bitter.

¹²And the fourth angel sounded, and the third part of the sun was smitten, and the third part of the moon, and the third part of the stars; so as the third part of them was darkened, and the day shone not for a third part of it, and the night likewise.

¹³And I beheld, and heard an angel flying through the midst of heaven, saying with a loud voice, Woe, woe, woe, to the inhabiters of the earth by reason of the other voices of the trumpet of the three angels, which are yet to sound!

In Chapter 8, the seventh seal is opened, and four of the seven trumpets it contains are sounded. We could speculate endlessly about whether or not the first four verses describe the heavenly equivalent of an ancient temple service, but I prefer not to get bogged down in such speculation. Whenever I start down the road toward making definitive statements about things which are open to subjective interpretation, a witticism of my grandfather's comes to mind; "that's more than a mule knows, and his head is longer than yours." It was a very succinct reminder that some things cannot be determined with certainty, regardless of how big your brain is, or how smart you are.

I believe it is sufficient to say that the first four trumpets bring a fresh batch of calamities. The calamity associated with the second trumpet is particularly interesting; *"and as it were a great mountain burning with fire was cast into the sea"*. Isn't this how you would expect someone who didn't have the word asteroid in his vocabulary to describe an asteroid strike? The surrounding calamities would also logically be associated with such an event. We don't need to know in advance whether this is an asteroid strike or some other event, we just need to be sufficiently grounded in scripture to put it in the proper context when it happens. Again, I go back to my assertion that if we are properly grounded in His word, God will reveal to us what we need to know, when we need to know it.

As a final note, I would suggest that the seven trumpets appear to be divided into two groups. The first four, here in Chapter 8, appear to be in rapid succession and perhaps related. The next three are announced as woeful, but appear to be more spaced out. Two are described in Chapter 9, and "the last trump" is announced with much fanfare in Chapter 10, but not actually sounded until Chapter 11. The "harvest" that follows "the last trump" is not described until Chapter 14. But, let's not get ahead of ourselves.

Revelation 9:1-21(KJV)

¹And the fifth angel sounded, and I saw a star fall from heaven unto the earth: and to him was given the key of the bottomless pit.

²And he opened the bottomless pit; and there arose a smoke out of the pit, as the smoke of a great furnace; and the sun and the air were darkened by reason of the smoke of the pit.

³And there came out of the smoke locusts upon the earth: and unto them was given power, as the scorpions of the earth have power.

⁴And it was commanded them that they should not hurt the grass of the earth, neither any green thing, neither any tree; but only those men which have not the seal of God in their foreheads.

⁵And to them it was given that they should not kill them, but that they should be tormented five months: and their torment was as the torment of a scorpion, when he striketh a man.

⁶And in those days shall men seek death, and shall not find it; and shall desire to die, and death shall flee from them.

⁷And the shapes of the locusts were like unto horses prepared unto battle; and on their heads were as it were crowns like gold, and their faces were as the faces of men.

8And they had hair as the hair of women, and their teeth were as the teeth of lions.

9And they had breastplates, as it were breastplates of iron; and the sound of their wings was as the sound of chariots of many horses running to battle.

10And they had tails like unto scorpions, and there were stings in their tails: and their power was to hurt men five months.

11And they had a king over them, which is the angel of the bottomless pit, whose name in the Hebrew tongue is Abaddon, but in the Greek tongue hath his name Apollyon.

12One woe is past; and, behold, there come two woes more hereafter.

13And the sixth angel sounded, and I heard a voice from the four horns of the golden altar which is before God,

14Saying to the sixth angel which had the trumpet, Loose the four angels which are bound in the great river Euphrates.

15And the four angels were loosed, which were prepared for an hour, and a day, and a month, and a year, for to slay the third part of men.

16And the number of the army of the horsemen were two hundred thousand thousand: and I heard the number of them.

17And thus I saw the horses in the vision, and them that sat on them, having breastplates of fire, and of jacinth, and brimstone: and the heads of the horses were as the heads of lions; and out of their mouths issued fire and smoke and brimstone.

18By these three was the third part of men killed, by the fire, and by the smoke, and by the brimstone, which issued out of their mouths.

19For their power is in their mouth, and in their tails: for their tails were like unto serpents, and had heads, and with them they do hurt.

20And the rest of the men which were not killed by these plagues yet repented not of the works of their hands, that they should not worship devils, and idols of gold, and silver, and brass, and stone, and of wood: which neither can see, nor hear, nor walk:

21Neither repented they of their murders, nor of their sorceries, nor of their fornication, nor of their thefts.

In the first verse of Chapter 9, we learn that "*star*" can be a reference to a being. This is instructive in terms of just how metaphorical some of these passages can be. It is pretty clear that this "being" unleashes the Devil and his minions on the earth.

Given the fact that this verse is very metaphorical, I believe we have permission to interpret the rest of the Chapter accordingly. Notice the reference to locusts and the comparison of same to horses. When he speaks of "locust" clad like horses prepared for battle, I have to wonder if John The Revelator might actually be describing helicopter gunships? Locust can fly. They have an exoskeleton; or external plates of armor if you will. Horses prepared for battle were clad in armor. Helicopter gunships are metal clad. Visualize a pilot and co-pilot, clad in a flight suit and helmet, behind the glass of a helicopter gunship coming straight at you. Now try to describe that scene using only words or terms from a 2000 year old vocabulary. The propellers could represent wings. Their helmets might be described as crowns (verse 7). Other aspects of their flight suits might be described as "*hair as the hair of women*" (verse 8); or his vision may have included female pilots. Their breathing and communication apparatus might be described as "teeth of lions" (verse 8). With just their faces above the glass and the metal nose of the helicopter appearing from the neck down, it's easy to see why he might describe them as having "breastplates of iron" (verse 9). The phrase "*and the sound of their wings was as the sound of chariots of many horses running to battle*" (verse 9), is an excellent description of the sound of a helicopter, even in today's terms. In verse 10 we find "*they had tails like unto scorpions*" and "*there were stings in their tails*". The missiles a helicopter launches originate more from the belly at mid-ship, but the smoke trail they emit make them appear to have been launched from the tail of the craft. Using a 2000 year old vocabulary, one would be hard pressed to come up with a more apt description of helicopter gunships than giant "*locusts*" with "*stings in their tails*" "*and the sound of their wings was as the sound of chariots of many horses running to battle*". If this was the vision John was given nearly 2000 years ago, his was a pretty apt description.

Whatever weapon or being John is describing, verse 11 makes it pretty clear that their commander is Satan. The fact that their rules of engagement do not include the right to kill (verse 5) at this point is also very interesting. It makes one think in terms of controlling masses of people through manipulation, pain, and terror.

In verse 13, the sixth trumpet is sounded, and the four "angels" (bent on destruction) that had been restrained until the sealing of the 144,000 (Rev 7:1-3) are now unleashed without constraint. They go forth with a 200 million man army (verse 16) and proceed to slay one third of the world population (verse 15). When I read the descriptions of the war machines, I think of tanks and armored personnel carriers. Again, modern words were not available to John. He used the vocabulary of his day.

I think there is a clue buried in the fact that the four angels were bound and subsequently loosed from "*the great river Euphrates*" (verse 14). These 4 angels might represent middle-eastern countries. I happen to believe the final conflict will be the descendants of Ismael (Islamist) versus the descendants of Isaac (Christians). The war will be fought over the Holy Land. But land is only one facet of the conflict. There are consequences for Abraham's impatience with God and taking matters into his own hands. It's not that God is vengeful or vindictive; it's just that in the natural course of things, wrong actions bring negative consequences. Consider ***Exodus 34:7(KJV)*** *⁷Keeping mercy for thousands, forgiving iniquity and transgression and sin, and that will by no means clear the guilty; visiting the iniquity of the fathers upon the children, and upon the children's children, unto the third and to the fourth generation.* People have to understand that God is loving, merciful, gracious, kind, and forgiving, but that doesn't mean we'll be spared the consequences of our misdeeds. If you jump off a cliff, God's graciousness isn't going to keep it from hurting when you hit the bottom. There is no conflict between the fact that God is loving, merciful, and gracious, and the fact that poor choices still have negative consequences. If this generation makes poor choices and bequeaths a morally and financially bankrupt society to our children, generations of them will pay the price for our insolence. The sins of the fathers are visited upon the children. That isn't vengeance; it's simply a natural consequence.

You may recall that when Lott fled the destruction of Sodom and Gomorrah and hid in the mountains with his daughters, they repeatedly got him drunk enough to have children by him (Gen

19). This incestuous relationship produced Moab and Ammon. A few generations later and for centuries thereafter, the descendants of Abraham were at war with the Moabites and Ammonites. There is no telling how many tens of thousands of their descendants paid with their lives for the sins of their ancestors. Poor choices have negative consequences that can go on for generations.

I don't mean to get off on a tangent. The point is that Abraham and Sarah may have made the mistake and paid a price in their own time; but the consequences (the conflicts between Isaac and Ismael, Christianity and Islam) have been playing out for centuries. I believe this conflict will be at the center of the events depicted in the book of Revelation. It will not be resolved until Christ returns. The descendants of Ismael will never concede their claim to the Holy Land by virtue of their status as descendants of the first born of Abraham. The descendants of Isaac will never concede by virtue of their status as descendants of the "child of promise". There will be no peace in the Middle East until it is initiated by the Prince of Peace. Don't misunderstand. That doesn't mean we shouldn't try; just as we must try to save as many individuals as possible from the great deception, even as we concede that the prophecy of a general falling away will prevail. We must likewise spare no effort in our quest for peace, even as we concede that peace will not prevail until Christ returns.

Revelation 10:1-11(KJV)
¹And I saw another mighty angel come down from heaven, clothed with a cloud: and a rainbow was upon his head, and his face was as it were the sun, and his feet as pillars of fire:
²And he had in his hand a little book open: and he set his right foot upon the sea, and his left foot on the earth,
³And cried with a loud voice, as when a lion roareth: and when he had cried, seven thunders uttered their voices.
⁴And when the seven thunders had uttered their voices, I was about to write: and I heard a voice from heaven saying unto me, Seal up those things which the seven thunders uttered, and write them not.
⁵And the angel which I saw stand upon the sea and upon the earth lifted up his hand to heaven,

⁶And sware by him that liveth for ever and ever, who created heaven, and the things that therein are, and the earth, and the things that therein are, and the sea, and the things which are therein, that there should be time no longer:

⁷But in the days of the voice of the seventh angel, when he shall begin to sound, the mystery of God should be finished, as he hath declared to his servants the prophets.

⁸And the voice which I heard from heaven spake unto me again, and said, Go and take the little book which is open in the hand of the angel which standeth upon the sea and upon the earth.

⁹And I went unto the angel, and said unto him, Give me the little book. And he said unto me, Take it, and eat it up; and it shall make thy belly bitter, but it shall be in thy mouth sweet as honey.

¹⁰And I took the little book out of the angel's hand, and ate it up; and it was in my mouth sweet as honey: and as soon as I had eaten it, my belly was bitter.

¹¹And he said unto me, Thou must prophesy again before many peoples, and nations, and tongues, and kings.

Bible commentaries differ as to the identity of the angel described in Chapter 10. Some maintain it is Christ Himself. No one knows for certain, but I believe it is Michael, the archangel. I take this position for several reasons. While the "being" here is obviously quite impressive; we don't see in this text the kind of language used to describe Jesus elsewhere in scripture, and more specifically we don't see the kind of language used just a few chapters earlier and later by this same writer. In addition, 1ˢᵗ Thessalonians 4:17 tells us the Lord's second coming will be announced by the archangel and Daniel tells us *"And at that time shall Michael stand up..."* (Dan 12:1). It seems to me this is what Revelation Chapter 10 is all about. Remember the context. This is after the sixth trumpet and before *"the last trump"*. In verse 7 we are told that *"in the days of the voice of the seventh angel, when he shall begin to sound, the mystery of God should be finished, as he hath declared to his servants the prophets."* Needless to say, the synthesis with all the related passages is clear. We can't be certain as to the time lapse involved, but we know all but "the last trump" has sounded and an angel has announced who and what to expect when it does.

Revelation 11:1-19(KJV)

1And there was given me a reed like unto a rod: and the angel stood, saying, Rise, and measure the temple of God, and the altar, and them that worship therein.

2But the court which is without the temple leave out, and measure it not; for it is given unto the Gentiles: and the holy city shall they tread under foot forty and two months.

3And I will give power unto my two witnesses, and they shall prophesy a thousand two hundred and threescore days, clothed in sackcloth.

4These are the two olive trees, and the two candlesticks standing before the God of the earth.

5And if any man will hurt them, fire proceedeth out of their mouth, and devoureth their enemies: and if any man will hurt them, he must in this manner be killed.

6These have power to shut heaven, that it rain not in the days of their prophecy: and have power over waters to turn them to blood, and to smite the earth with all plagues, as often as they will.

7And when they shall have finished their testimony, the beast that ascendeth out of the bottomless pit shall make war against them, and shall overcome them, and kill them.

8And their dead bodies shall lie in the street of the great city, which spiritually is called Sodom and Egypt, where also our Lord was crucified.

9And they of the people and kindreds and tongues and nations shall see their dead bodies three days and an half, and shall not suffer their dead bodies to be put in graves.

10And they that dwell upon the earth shall rejoice over them, and make merry, and shall send gifts one to another; because these two prophets tormented them that dwelt on the earth.

11And after three days and an half the Spirit of life from God entered into them, and they stood upon their feet; and great fear fell upon them which saw them.

12And they heard a great voice from heaven saying unto them, Come up hither. And they ascended up to heaven in a cloud; and their enemies beheld them.

13And the same hour was there a great earthquake, and the tenth part of the city fell, and in the earthquake were slain of men seven thousand: and the remnant were affrighted, and gave glory to the God of heaven.

[14] The second woe is past; and, behold, the third woe cometh quickly.
[15] And the seventh angel sounded; and there were great voices in heaven, saying, The kingdoms of this world are become the kingdoms of our Lord, and of his Christ; and he shall reign for ever and ever.
[16] And the four and twenty elders, which sat before God on their seats, fell upon their faces, and worshipped God,
[17] Saying, We give thee thanks, O Lord God Almighty, which art, and wast, and art to come; because thou hast taken to thee thy great power, and hast reigned.
[18] And the nations were angry, and thy wrath is come, and the time of the dead, that they should be judged, and that thou shouldest give reward unto thy servants the prophets, and to the saints, and them that fear thy name, small and great; and shouldest destroy them which destroy the earth.
[19] And the temple of God was opened in heaven, and there was seen in his temple the ark of his testament: and there were lightnings, and voices, and thunderings, and an earthquake, and great hail.

Verse 15 of Chapter 11 contains the long awaited *"last trump"*. The stage is now set for the second coming of Christ and the *"harvest of the earth"*. This chapter also speaks of two witnesses that God empowers to prophecy for 42 months. He then allows them to be killed by forces of the Antichrist. The whole world witnesses their bodies in the street for three and a half days before they are resurrected and called up to heaven. It isn't really germane to the point at hand, but I believe the two witnesses are the return of Enoch and Elijah. These two prophets of old did not experience death the first time around. They were translated from earth to heaven (Gen 5:24 and 2nd Kings 2:11). Hebrews 9:27 says; *"And as it is appointed unto men once to die, but after this the judgment:"* The Bible also tells us the wages of sin is death and all have sinned and come short of the glory of God. If Enoch and Elijah are the two witnesses, there are no exceptions to these passages of scripture.

I believe even those who are alive at the time of *"the harvest of the earth"* and are caught up to be with the Lord in the sky will experience death. I note that in the relevant passage (1st Corinthians 15:50-53), the Bible does not say we shall not all die. It says *"We shall not all sleep". ⁵⁰Now this I say, brethren, that flesh and blood cannot inherit the kingdom of God; neither doth corruption inherit incorruption. ⁵¹Behold, I show you a mystery; We shall not all sleep, but we shall all be changed, ⁵²In a moment, in the twinkling of an eye, at the last trump: for the trumpet shall sound, and the dead shall be raised incorruptible, and we shall be changed. ⁵³For this corruptible must put on incorruption, and this mortal must put on immortality.* The Bible consistently and repeatedly uses the word "sleep" to describe the state of being dead over time. Therefore, I take this passage to mean that we all must go through the process of exchanging mortality for immortality; exchanging a corruptible body for an incorruptible spirit. I know of no Biblical text for this being done except through death. At the same time, there are a number of passages declaring that death awaits us all. To paraphrase a few: the wages of sin is death; and so death passed upon all men for all have sinned; and it is appointed unto man once to die. When Paul said *"We shall not all sleep"*; I take that to mean that for believers who are alive for the *"harvest"*, there will be no state of being dead over time (sleep). Instead, there will be a momentary transformation (*in the twinkling of an eye*) from life, to death, to immortality. Needless to say, the mechanics of the transformation have no bearing on the more important question of timing. I only mention the mechanics because I believe the interpretation that cheats death is yet another example of doctrine based more on appeal than prayerful consideration.

The more germane point is that the death and resurrection of these two witnesses will be played out on the world stage and serve as a certain indicator that the "harvest" is at hand.

Revelation 12:1-17(KJV)
¹And there appeared a great wonder in heaven; a woman clothed with the sun, and the moon under her feet, and upon her head a crown of twelve stars: ²And she being with child cried, travailing in birth, and pained to be delivered.
³And there appeared another wonder in heaven; and behold a great red dragon, having seven heads and ten horns, and seven crowns upon his heads.

⁴And his tail drew the third part of the stars of heaven, and did cast them to the earth: and the dragon stood before the woman which was ready to be delivered, for to devour her child as soon as it was born.

⁵And she brought forth a man child, who was to rule all nations with a rod of iron: and her child was caught up unto God, and to his throne.

⁶And the woman fled into the wilderness, where she hath a place prepared of God, that they should feed her there a thousand two hundred and threescore days.

⁷And there was war in heaven: Michael and his angels fought against the dragon; and the dragon fought and his angels,

⁸And prevailed not; neither was their place found any more in heaven.

⁹And the great dragon was cast out, that old serpent, called the Devil, and Satan, which deceiveth the whole world: he was cast out into the earth, and his angels were cast out with him.

¹⁰And I heard a loud voice saying in heaven, Now is come salvation, and strength, and the kingdom of our God, and the power of his Christ: for the accuser of our brethren is cast down, which accused them before our God day and night.

¹¹And they overcame him by the blood of the Lamb, and by the word of their testimony; and they loved not their lives unto the death.

¹²Therefore rejoice, ye heavens, and ye that dwell in them. Woe to the inhabiters of the earth and of the sea! for the devil is come down unto you, having great wrath, because he knoweth that he hath but a short time.

¹³And when the dragon saw that he was cast unto the earth, he persecuted the woman which brought forth the man child.

¹⁴And to the woman were given two wings of a great eagle, that she might fly into the wilderness, into her place, where she is nourished for a time, and times, and half a time, from the face of the serpent.

¹⁵And the serpent cast out of his mouth water as a flood after the woman, that he might cause her to be carried away of the flood.

¹⁶And the earth helped the woman, and the earth opened her mouth, and swallowed up the flood which the dragon cast out of his mouth.

¹⁷And the dragon was wroth with the woman, and went to make war with the remnant of her seed, which keep the commandments of God, and have the testimony of Jesus Christ.

Our focus is on the question of timing for the *"harvest of the earth"*. Chapter 12 is very metaphorical, and only tangentially related to the question of timing. We won't dwell on it. It is an aside that offers perspective for events in the chapters around it. It speaks of Satan and his minions being cast out of heaven and how they persecuted God's chosen people from whom God brought forth the Messiah. It tells us Satan and his minions will *make war with the remnant of her seed*. It is continuing to set the stage for the now imminent "harvest" and final battle to come.

Revelation 13:1-18(KJV)
¹And I stood upon the sand of the sea, and saw a beast rise up out of the sea, having seven heads and ten horns, and upon his horns ten crowns, and upon his heads the name of blasphemy.
²And the beast which I saw was like unto a leopard, and his feet were as the feet of a bear, and his mouth as the mouth of a lion: and the dragon gave him his power, and his seat, and great authority.
³And I saw one of his heads as it were wounded to death; and his deadly wound was healed: and all the world wondered after the beast.
⁴And they worshipped the dragon which gave power unto the beast: and they worshipped the beast, saying, Who is like unto the beast? who is able to make war with him?
⁵And there was given unto him a mouth speaking great things and blasphemies; and power was given unto him to continue forty and two months.
⁶And he opened his mouth in blasphemy against God, to blaspheme his name, and his tabernacle, and them that dwell in heaven.
⁷And it was given unto him to make war with the saints, and to overcome them: and power was given him over all kindreds, and tongues, and nations.
⁸And all that dwell upon the earth shall worship him, whose names are not written in the book of life of the Lamb slain from the foundation of the world.
⁹If any man have an ear, let him hear.
¹⁰He that leadeth into captivity shall go into captivity: he that killeth with the sword must be killed with the sword. Here is the patience and the faith of the saints.

[11]And I beheld another beast coming up out of the earth; and he had two horns like a lamb, and he spake as a dragon.

[12]And he exerciseth all the power of the first beast before him, and causeth the earth and them which dwell therein to worship the first beast, whose deadly wound was healed.

[13]And he doeth great wonders, so that he maketh fire come down from heaven on the earth in the sight of men,

[14]And deceiveth them that dwell on the earth by the means of those miracles which he had power to do in the sight of the beast; saying to them that dwell on the earth, that they should make an image to the beast, which had the wound by a sword, and did live.

[15]And he had power to give life unto the image of the beast, that the image of the beast should both speak, and cause that as many as would not worship the image of the beast should be killed.

[16]And he causeth all, both small and great, rich and poor, free and bond, to receive a mark in their right hand, or in their foreheads:

[17]And that no man might buy or sell, save he that had the mark, or the name of the beast, or the number of his name.

[18]Here is wisdom. Let him that hath understanding count the number of the beast: for it is the number of a man; and his number is Six hundred threescore and six.

At the risk of being redundant, this book is not intended to be a commentary on the Bible. There are scores of those already available; some of them very good. I think most of them agree that the sea the beast rises up out of is the "sea" of humanity. The beast out of the sea is the Antichrist. The "dragon" from which he derives his power is Satan. The heads, horns, and crowns are said to represent countries and leaders with whom the Antichrist will be aligned. It appears that one of the "heads" will sustain a "deadly wound" from which it will miraculously recover; causing many that may have been on the fence to marvel after and worship the dragon and the beast. Needless to say, this is all very metaphorical. I don't believe anyone knows exactly what all of it means at this point. I do believe that if we stay grounded in scripture, we'll be able to correlate these events to the appropriate passages of scripture as they unfold. Cryptic metaphorical language is how God hides his plan from the lost, while letting his saints know what they need to know, when they need to know it. The covert war between good and evil, truth and deception, has been going on since Satan rebelled against God and was cast out of heaven for arrogance, pride, self-centeredness, insubordination, etc. (Isa. 14:12-15). The second beast of Revelation 13 will act as the high priest/prophet of the Antichrist. He will be capable of performing miracles to inspire people to follow the Antichrist. Those who conform to the will of the beast will take his mark in their hands or foreheads. Those who do not fall in line will be slaughtered. Needless to say, while the characters and timing may be somewhat nebulous at this point, when they begin to unfold, any student of scripture will know who the characters are and what is going to happen next. We'll know what we need to know, when we need to know it. When these events begin to unfold, the harvest will be imminent.

Revelation 14:1-20(KJV)

¹And I looked, and, lo, a Lamb stood on the mount Sion, and with him an hundred forty and four thousand, having his Father's name written in their foreheads.

²And I heard a voice from heaven, as the voice of many waters, and as the voice of a great thunder: and I heard the voice of harpers harping with their harps:

³And they sung as it were a new song before the throne, and before the four beasts, and the elders: and no man could learn that song but the hundred and forty and four thousand, which were redeemed from the earth.

⁴These are they which were not defiled with women; for they are virgins. These are they which follow the Lamb whithersoever he goeth. These were redeemed from among men, being the firstfruits unto God and to the Lamb.

⁵And in their mouth was found no guile: for they are without fault before the throne of God.

⁶And I saw another angel fly in the midst of heaven, having the everlasting gospel to preach unto them that dwell on the earth, and to every nation, and kindred, and tongue, and people,

⁷Saying with a loud voice, Fear God, and give glory to him; for the hour of his judgment is come: and worship him that made heaven, and earth, and the sea, and the fountains of waters.

8And there followed another angel, saying, Babylon is fallen, is fallen, that great city, because she made all nations drink of the wine of the wrath of her fornication.

9And the third angel followed them, saying with a loud voice, If any man worship the beast and his image, and receive his mark in his forehead, or in his hand,

10The same shall drink of the wine of the wrath of God, which is poured out without mixture into the cup of his indignation; and he shall be tormented with fire and brimstone in the presence of the holy angels, and in the presence of the Lamb:

11And the smoke of their torment ascendeth up for ever and ever: and they have no rest day nor night, who worship the beast and his image, and whosoever receiveth the mark of his name.

12Here is the patience of the saints: here are they that keep the commandments of God, and the faith of Jesus.

13And I heard a voice from heaven saying unto me, Write, Blessed are the dead which die in the Lord from henceforth: Yea, saith the Spirit, that they may rest from their labours; and their works do follow them.

14And I looked, and behold a white cloud, and upon the cloud one sat like unto the Son of man, having on his head a golden crown, and in his hand a sharp sickle.

15And another angel came out of the temple, crying with a loud voice to him that sat on the cloud, Thrust in thy sickle, and reap: for the time is come for thee to reap; for the harvest of the earth is ripe.

16And he that sat on the cloud thrust in his sickle on the earth; and the earth was reaped.

17And another angel came out of the temple which is in heaven, he also having a sharp sickle.

18And another angel came out from the altar, which had power over fire; and cried with a loud cry to him that had the sharp sickle, saying, Thrust in thy sharp sickle, and gather the clusters of the vine of the earth; for her grapes are fully ripe.

19And the angel thrust in his sickle into the earth, and gathered the vine of the earth, and cast it into the great winepress of the wrath of God.

20And the winepress was trodden without the city, and blood came out of the winepress, even unto the horse bridles, by the space of a thousand and six hundred furlongs.

Perhaps now you understand why I began this chapter with the obligatory statement that the word "rapture" does not appear in the Bible. Even so, I do not question the concept of the church being "raptured". I just prefer to use the word "*harvested*" or the phrase "*harvest of the earth*" because, unlike "rapture", the precise phrase "*harvest of the earth*" does appear in the appropriate context in scripture and the analogy to farming runs throughout the entire Old and New Testaments. Christ Himself used The Parable Of The Wheats And The Tares to illustrate how the saved and lost would be intertwined until the harvest; at which time they would be separated, with the wheat gathered into His barn and the tares being burned. So there is no disagreement on the concept of the church being harvested, and I wouldn't quibble with the terminology one uses to express the concept. The question has always been about the timing.

I think any reasonable person would have to agree that an event as cataclysmic as the "*harvest of the earth*" (or rapture if you prefer) would have to be described in some detail in the scripture. There has to be a body of text one can point to and say; here is described the events known as the "*harvest of the earth*", or rapture if you prefer. After all, the Bible does record events from creation to final judgment, including events of arguably much less importance. So, Biblically speaking, when and where does this "*harvest of the earth*" take place? If you have studied the above passages, you know the short answer is it takes place toward the end of the Great Tribulation period, as recorded for us in Revelation Chapter 14 and surrounding text. The precise phrase "*harvest of the earth*" is lifted directly from Revelation 14:15.

In the Old Testament we find numerous references to the "first fruits" of the harvest being presented as a "wave offering" unto God by the high priest. Perhaps the best example is in Leviticus 23:10-11; *[10]Speak unto the children of Israel, and say unto them, When ye be come into the land which I give unto you, and shall reap the harvest thereof, then ye shall bring a sheaf of the firstfruits of your harvest unto the priest: [11]And he shall wave the sheaf before the LORD, to be accepted for you....* In Revelation 14:1- we see a picture of Christ (our high Priest), presenting on the high and holy ground of Mount

Zion, one hundred forty-four thousand of the best people the earth has produced as a wave offering *unto God and to the Lamb* of the <u>*firstfruits*</u> of the *"harvest of the earth."* This isn't rocket science and it doesn't involve speculation. Revelation 14:1 speaks of *"a Lamb"*. Could that be other than THE High Priest, Jesus Christ? In verse 4, the one hundred forty-four thousand are described as *"being the firstfruits unto God…"*. And in verses 14-16 *the earth is ripe* and the harvest is *reaped* by the *Son of man* on a *white cloud*. Obviously, the events described in the early verses of Revelation 14 are precursors to a harvest and perfectly consistent with the teachings going all the way back to Exodus and Leviticus. The references to the *Son of man* coming on a *cloud* are found in Matthew 24:30, Revelation 14:14-16, and 1st Thessalonians 4:17, to name only the most notable. The scene will ring bells with even the occasional church goer. One doesn't have to be a student of eschatology to see the second coming of Christ and the *"harvest of the earth"* in Chapter 14 of Revelation. But we are still zeroing in on the question of timing.

The above interpretation of Revelation 14 is also perfectly compatible with the Parable Of The Wheats And The Tares (Mt 13:24-30 & 37-43). In this parable Christ taught that good and evil would co-exist until the *Son of man shall send forth his angels.* He went on to say *the harvest is the end of the world;* at which time *the tares* will be *gathered and burned in the fire.* In Revelation 14:10 we see those who have taken the mark of the beast *"tormented with fire and brimstone…"* The Son of man teaming up with the angels and carrying out the harvest is depicted in Revelation 14:15-19. It's easy to see how Leviticus 23:10 and Matthew 13 dovetail with Revelation 14.

Obviously, the idea of the *"harvest of the earth"* ("rapture") depicted in Revelation 14 is consistent with the broader context of Biblical teaching. Having established that, let's move on to the details of very specific prerequisites to the second coming and *"harvest of the earth."* In dealing with specifics there is no better place to begin than with the teachings of Christ Himself. Just as we looked to His Parable Of The Wheats And The Tares for general context, we can look at His specific teachings on eschatology for details.

In what is known as the Olivet Discourse in Matthew chapter 24, Jesus responds to a question put to Him by His disciples; *"when shall these things be? and what shall be the sign of thy coming, and of the end of the world?"* What follows is about all one needs to know about eschatology. In verses 4 through 8 Jesus tells them, and us, to take heed lest we be deceived. He indicates that many will come claiming to be Christ. There will be wars and rumors of wars, with nations and kingdoms rising against each other. There will be famines, pestilences, and earthquakes in diverse places. These are but the *"beginning of sorrows"*.

In verse 9, with regard to Christians, He points out *"they shall deliver you up to be afflicted, and shall kill you: and ye shall be hated of all nations for my name's sake."* Please compare this to Revelation Chapter 6, where in preparation for the final judgment, Christ begins to break open the seven seals on the "Lambs Book Of Life". With the breaking of the first four seals come the "four horsemen of the apocalypse" with wars, famines, pestilences, death, and destruction. A massive earthquake is associated with the opening of the sixth seal. This seems to be a perfect correlation to the "beginning of sorrows". Remember there is another seal to be opened and seven trumpets to be blown to finish setting the stage for the *"harvest of the earth"*.

I don't see anything up to this point about believers being spared tribulation. Indeed, in verse 10 of Revelation Chapter 6, we see the saints that have been martyred up to that point pleading with Christ to avenge their blood. Christ responds by offering them comfort, while also telling them they must wait for tribulation to further separate the wheat from the chafe, which will involve the martyrdom of additional saints. It seems obvious the saints have not been harvested (raptured) at this point.

Now, let's turn back to Matthew 24 and the Olivet Discourse. Picking back up at Matthew 24:11, Jesus predicts that *many false prophets shall rise, and shall deceive many.* This is the underlying thesis of this book. I believe those who are preaching the "easybelieveism", "eternal security", "prosperity theology", and "escapeism" are false prophets that are setting the stage for mass desertion when the proverbial ship hits the sand. We do not brace for trials, or develop the steely resolve we need to get through hardship, by looking at the future through rose colored glasses. In Matthew 24:12 Jesus states it thusly *"And because iniquity shall abound, the love of many shall wax cold."* Love waxing cold could also be described as a "falling away".

Speaking of the same end time events, the Apostle Paul says in 2nd Thessalonians Chapter 2 verses 1 through 4 *¹Now we beseech you, brethren, by the coming of our Lord Jesus Christ, and by our gathering together unto him, ²That ye be not soon shaken in mind, or be troubled, neither by spirit, nor by word, nor by letter as from us, as that the day of Christ is at hand. ³Let no man deceive you by any means: for that day shall not come, except there come a falling away first, and that man of sin be revealed, the son of perdition; ⁴Who opposeth and exalteth himself above all that is called God, or that is worshipped; so that he as God sitteth in the temple of God, showing himself that he is God.* Paul is putting down a marker that Jesus' *"harvest of the earth"* will not take place until there has been a *"falling away first"* and the Antichrist is revealed. This *"falling away"* is what I'm trying to help individuals avoid. The prophecies of the Old Testament, Christ, Paul and others can't be overturned. When tribulation befalls the church, many will depart from the faith because they are being coddled instead of challenged; they are having their ears tickled instead of being fed a steady diet of truth. As a group, the church will experience a mass exodus of the fair weather faithful. That does not mean that you and I, as individuals, have to be among the fallen. If we are aware of the signs and the timeline to the degree that we understand what is happening and we are hardened in our resolve, having no delusions about it being easy, we should be able to *"endure unto the end"*, and *"be saved."* You may notice this last phraseology was lifted directly from Jesus' Olivet Discourse as recorded in Matthew 24:13. Again, take note that no passage is talking about the saints being exempt from tribulation. Salvation is the reward of those who, if called upon, *"endure unto the end"*.

In Matthew 24:14 Jesus says, *"And this gospel of the kingdom shall be preached in all the world for a witness unto all nations; and then shall the end come."* This provides another marker. We know the gospel message must reach the entire world before the *harvest*. With the invention and widespread use of television, in a sense, we could say this milestone has already been reached. Even so, I'm keeping an eye out for an additional sign. As the events of the *harvest* are beginning to unfold in Revelation 14, in verse 6 the writer *"saw another angel fly in the midst of heaven, having the everlasting gospel to preach unto them that dwell on the earth, and to every nation, and kindred, and tongue, and people."* One gets the sense the writer is speaking of an event rather than a time frame and the fact that *"angel"* is singular, leads me to suspect this might be a single event, or series of events, involving a single individual. I get the same sense from reading the corresponding passage in Matthew 24:14. I've heard speculation that the *"angel"* might be the Rev. Billy Graham. An argument can certainly be made that he has reached the world with the gospel. Fortunately, I don't feel that one needs to take a definitive stand one way or another on this issue at this time. It is one of many markers. I'm content to temporarily set this issue aside, assuming that future considerations will be illuminated by additional revelations.

In Matthew 24 verses 15 through 21, Jesus tells us how we will know when we have passed from the *"beginning of sorrows"* into the period of *"great tribulation"*; a period *"such as was not since the beginning of the world to this time, no, nor ever shall be."* He tells us in verse 15 that *"When ye therefore shall see the ABOMINATION OF DESOLATION, spoken of by Daniel the prophet, stand in the holy place"*, then you will know the ship has hit the sand and all hell is about to break loose. Jesus notes in Matthew 24:22 that things will get so bad that if God didn't intervene, the destruction might be total. There might not be any survivors. The corresponding Revelation passage is in Chapter 13 verses 4 through 8. *"⁴And they worshipped the dragon which gave power unto the beast: and they worshipped the beast, saying, Who is like unto the beast? who is able to make war with him? ⁵And there was given unto him a mouth speaking great things and blasphemies; and power was given unto him to continue forty and two months. ⁶And he opened his mouth in blasphemy against God, to blaspheme his name, and his tabernacle, and them that dwell in heaven. ⁷And it was given unto him* to make war with the saints, and to overcome them: and power was given him over all kindreds, and tongues, and nations. *And all that dwell upon the earth shall worship him, whose names are not written in the book of life of the Lamb slain from the foundation of the world."* Note that in verse 24 of Matthew Chapter 24 (*24For there shall arise false Christs, and false prophets, and shall show great signs and wonders; insomuch that, if it were possible, they shall deceive the very elect.*) and in verses 7 and 8 of Revelation 13, the saints/elect are still here on earth fighting the good fight. Clearly, they have not been harvested into God's barn yet. He is still using tribulation to separate the wheat from the chaff before gathering the former into his barn and burning the latter. This is also consistent with the passage in Daniel 11:31-36 that Jesus refers to in Matthew 24:15. Daniel tells us in 11:33 and 35 that *"they that understand among the people shall instruct many; yet they shall fall by the sword, and by flame, by captivity, and by spoil..."* He goes on to say; *"some of them of understanding shall fall, to try them, and to purge, and to make them white, even to the time of the end:...."* It would seem that Daniel's point is that no one, not even those of complete understanding, will be spared the consequences of man's self-destructive behavior.

In Matthew 24:26, Jesus tells us not to be taken in by those who might claim the second coming has occurred and try to point us toward Him. In verse 27 He indicates there will be nothing subtle about His return. *"27For as the lightning cometh out of the east, and shineth even unto the west; so shall also the coming of the Son of man be."* Finally, the most definitive statement regarding the relative timing of the "harvest" is made in Matthew 24:29-30; *"29Immediately after the tribulation of those days shall the sun be darkened, and the moon shall not give her light, and the stars shall fall from heaven, and the powers of the heavens shall be shaken: 30And then shall appear the sign of the Son of man in heaven: and then shall all the tribes of the earth mourn, and they shall see the Son of man coming in the clouds of heaven with power and great glory. 31And he shall send his angels with a great sound of a trumpet, and they shall gather together his elect from the four winds, from one end of heaven to the other."* Please note the phrases *"after the tribulation"* and *"then shall appear the sign of the Son of man in heaven*". It is hard to imagine clearer language than this. The timing of the "*harvest*" is "*after the tribulation*" period that is portrayed in the first 13 chapters of Revelation. Please follow how this dovetails with other scripture in the next several paragraphs.

You will notice that in Matthew 24:31, His coming will be with the sound of a trumpet; (*And he shall send his angels with a great sound of a trumpet.*) This isn't just any trumpet. In speaking of the transformation from mortal to immortal that will take place when we are "harvested" (or raptured if you prefer), Paul tells us in 1st Corinthians 15:52 that it will take place "*at the last trump*". This is critically important. In terms of eschatology, there is only one "last trump". You may recall that the tribulation period began in Revelation 6:1 with the "*Lamb*" beginning to open the seven seals on the Book of Life. The breaking of each seal marked the beginning of a new tribulation. The seventh seal, the opening of which is recorded in Revelation 8:1, results in seven angels being given seven trumpets. The sounding of each of these trumpets (between Rev 8:7 & Rev 11:15), in turn, signaled a new calamity. The "*last*" of these trumpets is sounded in Revelation 11:15; *15And the seventh angel sounded; and there were great voices in heaven, saying, The kingdoms of this world are become the kingdoms of our Lord, and of his Christ; and he shall reign for ever and ever.*

I know that when one tries to tie together and synthesize all the related passages, it is easy to get lost in the tall grass. It's sort of like trying to make out a crop circle pattern from the ground. To get a really clear picture one has to look at an overview. That's what I hope to offer in the following chart where the eschatological teachings of Christ, Daniel, and Paul are reduced to a checklist with references to the text of fulfillment.

Text And Prediction	Fulfilled
Mt 24:4-11 & Dan Chapters 11 & 12 Wars, Famines, Pestilence, Quakes…	Rev Chapters 5 – 8
Dan 12:1 & Matthew 24:21 Great Tribulation	Rev Chapters 9-13
Mt 24:12 & 2nd Thessalonians 2:3 A "falling away" from the faith	Revelation 13:4-5
Dan 11:31, Mt 24:15 & 2nd Thes 2:3 Abomination & Antichrist Revealed	Revelation 13
Dan 11:32, Mt 24:23-24 & 2nd Thes 2:1-12 The Great Deception	Revelation 13:14
Matthew 24:12 Gospel Preached Worldwide	Revelation 14:6
Mt 24:31, 1st Cor 15:52, 1st Thes 4:17 & Rev 10:7 The (last) Trump	Revelation 11:15
Mt 24:30, 1st Thes 4:17 & Mk 13:26 Christ Appearing In Clouds/Heavens	Revelation 14:15
Mt 13:24-30 &36-43, Mt 24:31 The Earth Harvested	Rev 14:15-20

I should note that the preceding chart is not meant to be exhaustive. There are many other prophecies that find fulfillment in the Book of Revelation. I left out many of the more subtle ones for the sake of clarity. Likewise I left out repetitive accounts of the Olivet Discourse in the Gospels of Mark and Luke.

Given this body of evidence, it is difficult to comprehend anyone placing the *"harvest of the earth"* anywhere but Revelation 14. However, those who hold a pre-tribulation rapture position cannot place it in Revelation 14 and still maintain their position. At the same time they cannot dispute the fact that an event as cataclysmic as the "harvest", or rapture, has to be recorded in the Bible; the book that records everything from creation to final judgment. The mental and verbal contortions they will indulge, and try to foist upon the rest of us in order to place the *"harvest"* before the "tribulation period", are amazingly audacious. I think they subconsciously understand how weak their argument is. I've not known any to volunteer the text their pre-trib belief forces them to rely on. If called upon to cite the specific text, they are almost certain to point to Revelation 4:1. *After this I looked, and, behold, a door was opened in heaven: and the first voice which I heard was as it were of a trumpet talking with me; which said, Come up hither, and I will show thee things which must be hereafter.* It is pretty clear from Revelation 4:1 and the surrounding text that John is being called up to heaven and allowed to see the future he describes in the rest of the Book of Revelation.

Revelation 4:1 is not preceded by the prerequisites we are told to look for and the text itself does not contain the trappings of a "harvest", "rapture", or second coming. There has been no tribulation; no Antichrist; no two witnesses, no gospel preached throughout the world; no mark of the Beast; no "falling away"; no Christ in the clouds; no angels; and no "last trump". Despite these glaring shortcomings, proponents of the pre-tribulation "rapture" are forced to grasp at the straw of Revelation 4:1. They cannot acknowledge the perfect fit of Revelation 14 and still credibly maintain their pre-tribulation "rapture" position. Sadly, many have compromised their credibility, and the sanctity of the Word, by contorting the scripture in an effort to maintain their pre-trib position.

The list of scriptures that have to be ignored, explained away, downplayed, or manipulated in order to place the *"harvest of the earth"* in Revelation 4:1 is quite extensive. Perhaps even more amazing is the interpretation of Revelation 14 one is forced to come up with if the "harvest" (rapture) is placed in Revelation 4:1. Since Revelation 14 is chronologically in the right place, all the prerequisites are in place, and the language is so clear it can't be explained away; those who hold the pre-trib position are forced to take the position that Revelation 14 is second coming number two! I know this seems self-contradictory on its face; but since they cannot dispute the coming of Christ in Revelation 14 or the fact that it is after the tribulation period, their only option is to attempt to finesse it by insisting there are actually two second comings; one in Revelation 4:1 where He comes for the saints, and one in Revelation 14 where He returns with the saints. Regardless of how one attempts to finesse it, there simply is no Biblical basis for the suggestion of two second comings or for Revelation 4 being the description of one of those comings. None of the events associated with the second coming of Christ are present in Revelation 4. There is only one text where all the spelled out prerequisites have been met and the events described match the events predicted. That text is Revelation 14.

What could drive people to such mental and verbal contortions? Why go to such extremes to avoid the clear meaning of the text? The Parable Of The Wheats And The Tares (Mt 13:24-30 & 36-43) and The Olivet Discourse (Mt 24) are not difficult to understand. These two passages contain some of the clearest language in scripture. Consider Matthew 24 verses 29 and 30; *29Immediately **after the tribulation** of those days shall the sun be darkened, and the moon shall not give her light, and the stars shall fall from heaven, and the powers of the heavens shall be shaken: 30And **then shall appear the sign of the Son of man** in heaven: and then shall all the tribes of the earth mourn, and they shall see the Son of man coming in the clouds of heaven with power and great glory.* To remove all potential for misunderstanding as it relates to the Parable Of The Wheats And The Tares, Christ Himself explains it for us in Matthew 24:36-43.

Regrettably, we're left with no pleasant option in answering the question of what drives people to such extremes in their effort to avoid the obvious interpretation of when the *"harvest of the earth"* takes place. For those who do not study the Word, you can chalk it up to a lack of interest and/or poor scholarship, with or without taking it to the level of questioning the reason for the lack of interest. On the other hand, students of scripture can't fall back on the excuse of poor scholarship. For them, maintaining the self-contradictory position of two second comings and placing the "rapture" in Revelation 4:1 where there is no contextual support requires a level of delusion. Note; I am not saying they are necessarily stupid, bad, or evil, just delusional. Delusion is loosely defined as a belief that is held despite indisputable evidence to the contrary. Delusion occurs when the warm fuzzy feeling we get from the preferred belief is more important to us than truth. God said he would send *"strong delusion"* to those who *"received not the love of the truth"*.

I've heard all the arguments the proponents of "escapeism" (pre-tribulation "rapture") have to offer. "The Olivet Discourse was not meant for us." "It was meant only for the disciples He was addressing." If that were so, the whole Bible could be negated on the same basis. What good is a Bible if its pages can be rendered blank by interpretation? By the same token, if a major event can be read into an unrelated passage, what good is it? If one can read all the prerequisites and the entire *"harvest of the earth"* into Revelation 4:1, there is no limit to what one can "read into" any passage of scripture. If one can negate entire chapters by essentially saying "He wasn't talking to me", and read into other verses long descriptive narratives that simply aren't there, the Bible can be made to say anything one wants it to say. One cannot ignore clear language and abandon common sense in order to maintain a pleasant but unsupported position without acknowledging a level of delusion is at work.

A reprint of 2nd Thessalonians Chapter 2, verses 1 through 12 is probably in order. *¹Now we beseech you, brethren, by the coming of our Lord Jesus Christ, and by our gathering together unto him, ²That ye be not soon shaken in mind, or be troubled, neither by spirit, nor by word, nor by letter as from us, as that the day of Christ is at hand. ³Let no man deceive you by any means: for that day shall not come, except there come a falling away first, and that man of sin be revealed, the son of perdition; ⁴Who opposeth and exalteth himself above all that is called God, or that is worshipped; so that he as God sitteth in the temple of God, showing himself that he is God. ⁵Remember ye not, that, when I was yet with you, I told you these things? ⁶And now ye know what withholdeth that he might be revealed in his time. ⁷For the mystery of iniquity doth already work: only he who now letteth will let, until he be taken out of the way. ⁸And then shall that Wicked be revealed, whom the Lord shall consume with the spirit of his mouth, and shall destroy with the brightness of his coming: ⁹Even him, whose coming is after the working of Satan with all power and signs and lying wonders, ¹⁰And with all deceivableness of unrighteousness in them that <u>perish; because they received not the love of the truth</u>, that they might be saved. ¹¹And <u>for this cause God shall send them strong delusion</u>, that they should believe a lie: ¹²That they all might be damned who believed not the truth, but had pleasure in unrighteousness.* I guess my point, and the point of this text is that in the end, we will either be immersed in seeking the truth, or we will become victims of our own delusions.

Now before anyone jumps to conclusions, I am not trying to elevate views on eschatology to the status of determining ones salvation. Clearly, people can hold a pre-tribulation "rapture" view and still be saved. I'm not questioning their salvation. I am questioning their scholarship, commitment to truth, and resolve. I am suggesting that those who hold this view will be in for an awfully rude awakening if they find themselves in the tribulation period mentally, spiritually, and theologically unprepared. I would also suggest that in this condition, they would be infinitely more likely to be among those who "fall away" from the faith during these trials. As noted earlier, I feel like my mission is to help people mentally, spiritually, and theologically prepare for the tribulation I believe we are promised in our individual lives as well as the collective "Tribulation Period" the church will face before the "*harvest*".

I don't focus on these issues because of any animus. I don't take any pleasure in challenging the beliefs of others. The path of least resistance is to hold on to my own beliefs and let others have theirs. At the same time, I can't remain silent in the face of the propagation of doctrines I believe are undermining the resolve of the saints and setting the church up for the "falling away" predicted in scripture. I know I can't prevent the falling away because it is predicted, but I may be able to help individuals avoid the consequences by pointing them toward truth. In Chapter 11, verses 33 through 35, Daniel tells us those who understand will instruct many. Even though they and the instructors may succumb, they will be helped nonetheless. As has been noted many times, God doesn't promise us a life without storms, He just promises to be with us during those storms.

The idea that we can be transported from hedonism to heaven on a feather bed is the essence of "itching ears theology". The four cornerstones of "itching ears theology" we have covered so far are "easybelieveism", "eternal security", "prosperity theology", and "escapeism". I want to call the church to account for these dubious doctrines.

Chapter Six

"Meism"

"Meism" is the title I've assigned to self-centeredness / narcissism, the disease that underlies all "isms". The common thread that runs through all the dubious doctrines the church is teaching is the fact that they are all self-serving; that is to say, they sustain the church; feather the nests of the ministers who lead it; and tickle the ears of the listeners. The doctrines we've talked about in earlier chapters make it easier for the church to attract attendees. They have generally been more subtle and collective in their approach. With "meism", we're moving into the realm of doctrines that make it easier for the church to separate the attendees from their money. The doctrines we'll talk about in the next couple of chapters are perhaps a little less subtle and targeted more toward the individual. But first, let's examine the aspect of human nature that motivates both the con artist and his mark.

Speaking to the priestly class of the day, In Malachi 1:10 God asked the rhetorical question, *Who is there even among you that would shut the doors for nought?* His point was that if they weren't being compensated for it, they'd abandon their post and wouldn't even bother to close the doors on their way out. From this we get the truism that "no one does nought but for gain". It is not so much a condemnation as it is a simple statement of fact about human nature. It has been so from the dawn of time. Self-centeredness was the original sin; the one that got Satan expelled from heaven. We learn about it in Isaiah 14:12-15; *12How art thou fallen from heaven, O Lucifer, son of the morning! how art thou cut down to the ground, which didst weaken the nations! 13For thou hast said in thine heart, I will ascend into heaven, I will exalt my throne above the stars of God: I will sit also upon the mount of the congregation, in the sides of the north: 14I will ascend above the heights of the clouds; I will be like the most High. 15Yet thou shalt be brought down to hell, to the sides of the pit.* Note that in two verses the Devil uses the phrase "I will" five times. One does not have to have great interpretive skills or a degree in psychology to see the self-centeredness that underlies those statements.

Likewise, the fall of mankind is all about self-centeredness. Eve, and later Adam, didn't partake of the forbidden fruit because they were hungry; they were motivated to indulge by the pursuit of self-aggrandizement. Note Genesis 3:4-6 *And the serpent said unto the woman, Ye shall not surely die: 5For God doth know that in the day ye eat thereof, then your eyes shall be opened, and ye shall be as gods, knowing good and evil. 6And when the woman saw that the tree was good for food, and that it was pleasant to the eyes, and a tree to be desired to make one wise, she took of the fruit thereof, and did eat, and gave also unto her husband with her; and he did eat.* Again, we see the desire to promote self-interest at work.

Self-centeredness; is the sin we inherit from Adam; the sin into which we are conceived. *Wherefore, as by one man sin entered into the world, and death by sin; and so death passed upon all men, for that all have sinned:* (Romans 5:12) We are born self-centered. Babies know nothing of sharing, empathy, or sympathy. Their only concern is self. But, far be it for me to pick on babies when I can let the Bible do it for me. David told us in Psalm 51:5, *Behold, I was shapen in iniquity, and in sin did my mother conceive me.* David, a man after God's own heart, knew he was the product of self-seeking and that self-centeredness was in his DNA. The thing that set David apart, is the fact that he understood the depths of his depravity, and thus his need for grace and a savior. Genesis 8:21 tells us that we are predisposed toward evil from childhood. The evil spoken of here is evil in the sense that, from the earliest age, every inclination we have is toward self-promotion. Even when we grow up and learn to constrain our base instincts to some degree, it's often just a matter of becoming more subtle and getting better at disguising our pursuit of self-interest. In fact, we often become so good at it, we can fool ourselves into thinking our motives are pure. This is where Jeremiah 17:9 comes in; *The heart is deceitful above all things, and desperately wicked: who can know it?* Even when we mourn the tragic and untimely loss of a loved one, the grief is over our loss and the impact it will have on us. When we give, how many of us give without thought to how we might ultimately benefit, in this life or the next? Do some soul-searching before you answer that question.

Self-centeredness is also practiced on a corporate scale; that is to say, groups of all sizes can fall collectively into the trap. The history of Israel is replete with examples of putting aside God's plan in the pursuit of self-interest. No individual or group is exempt. *All we like sheep have gone astray; we have turned every one to his own way; and the LORD hath laid on him the iniquity of us all* (Is 53:6) Church history is also full of self-serving doctrines, such as the practice of selling indulgences.

These are not new revelations. Self-centeredness was the sin that drove Satan out of heaven. It was the sin that drove Adam and Eve out of the garden. It was the sin that drove the nation of Israel repeatedly into captivity. It is the sin that is driving the church of today toward the "doctrines of devils", just as it did the church of Jesus' day. It is the sin that motivates all of us. It will be the sin that motivates the Antichrist. Only one person in history ever gained complete victory over self-centeredness. That person was Christ. He modeled for us a lifetime of self-sacrifice. Everything he did was to the benefit of others. We will not achieve that level of victory as long as we have the cross of flesh to bear; but through Him, we can experience the unspeakable joy of escaping the bonds of self for fleeting moments.

The point, in this context, is that anyone who says their motives are entirely pure is ignorant, delusional, or lying. Make no mistake; self-centeredness is the soil that nourishes the root of all evil. Paul tells us in 1st Timothy 6:10, *"For the love of money is the root of all evil..."* That is certainly true. But let's take it a step further. Why do people love money? It isn't for its intrinsic beauty; it has none. We love it because we can use it to lavish gifts on ourselves. Putting it another way, we love money because it can purchase things that can be laid on the altar before the god of self. Why do you think Paul said *"covetousness...is idolatry"* (Col 3:5)? Idolatry, by definition requires an idol. Self is the idol of which Paul speaks when he says *"covetousness...is idolatry"*. It explains why "thou shalt not covet" is among the Ten Commandments. Perhaps, it is why the ten begin with "thou shalt have no other gods before me" and end with "thou shalt not covet". It closes the loop. The love of money may be the root of all evil, but self-centeredness is the soil from which the root draws its nourishment and without which evil cannot survive.

The doctrines we've looked at in earlier chapters serve the broad purpose of bringing supporters on board and thus insuring the survival of the denomination as well as the church and its' leaders; at least in terms of numbers, if not in mission. As such, they are self-serving in a broad corporate sense.

Now that we've taken a broad view of how "meism" permeates everything we do, individually and collectively, let's look at a specific church doctrine that serves the self-interest of the corporate church and the individuals who lead it in a more direct way.

CHAPTER SEVEN

Tithing

THE WORD "TITHE" APPEARS 11 times in the Old Testament (KJV). It appears twice in the New Testament (KJV). Both instances in the New Testament are the gospel accounts (Mt 23:23 & Lk 11:42) of a single instance whereby Jesus chastises the Pharisees for tithing down to the most trivial of things while neglecting the weightier matters of love and justice. He notes that the tithing was appropriate, but explicitly downplays its relative importance. I don't pretend to know the mind of God, but perhaps this is because the theocracy that tithing was established to support, had waxed and waned along with the history of His people. At times, the nation of Israel was so scattered and assimilated into the culture of their captors that the theocracy didn't exist, thus there was no institution to collect or make use of the tithe. At the time of Christ, the Jewish state existed, but not independently or as a complete theocracy. They were under Roman rule. As such, Rome allowed them to practice their religion and maintain some semblance of their old justice system; but Roman law was supreme and they obviously wouldn't be allowed to raise or support their own army. As such, the money needed to finance functions the Jewish state was still allowed to carry out was diminished. This would certainly explain the complete absence of emphasis on tithing in the New Testament. Conversely, to the extent that government services were now provided by the Romans, early Jews and Christians were forced to support these functions by way of a tax paid to the emperor. You may recall, the Pharisees tried to trick Christ with a question about the legality of paying taxes (Mt 22:15-21). His response was classic: holding up a coin with the image of Caesar and a Roman inscription he proclaimed, *Render therefore unto Caesar the things which are Caesar's; and unto God the things that are God's.*

God selected His people, organized them under a theocracy, and instituted the 10% tithe as a means of supporting the leaders, administering justice, building and maintaining infrastructure, and providing for the common defense. As noted earlier, there have been many times, some very protracted, when the people of Israel did not exist as a nation. There have also been times when the nation existed in name, but was under the rule of other nations. It is an unfortunate fact that God's plan for government and the financing of same has been relegated to the dust bin of history, for at least the time being. The only theocracies left in the world are a few Islamic countries led by their Ayatollahs. For better or worse, since we're not a theocracy in the Old Testament sense, the functions of state no longer have to be financed out of the tithe. So...if the state and the functions of defense, infrastructure, and courts are supported by other means, the tithe of 10% should be well in excess of what is needed to support just the church. Perhaps if the church still fulfilled the role of supplying the needy, the 10% could still be justified; but the government that now takes 40% of what we earn has assumed that role as well. I believe the church and the state share equally in the blame for government assuming the role of charity. I further believe they both had their own self-centered reasons. The government bureaucrats saw it as a way to build their kingdoms and churches saw it as a way to free up resources that could be used to pay themselves more and improve their facilities.

In light of the absence of a theocracy, the absence of New Testament teaching on the subject, and the church's diminished role in so many areas, why do so many ministers and churches still place so much emphasis on the 10% tithe? This question pretty much answers itself. Ministers and churches place an inordinate amount of emphasis on tithing because ministers and churches are the primary beneficiaries of tithing. It's no more complicated than that. If tithing were based strictly on the diminished role of the modern church, as opposed to the desires of that particular minister or assembly, the emphasis and amount would both be adjusted downward.

Obviously, God was right in that 10% is an adequate amount to finance all the functions of both church and state, if both are well managed. Ten percent dedicated to just paying the preacher and maintaining the church is a tremendous windfall in a church of any significant size. That's why the buildings end up being so opulent and the ministers so handsomely paid. In smaller churches where there is no economy of scale, they are barely making ends meet. Unfortunately, the smaller churches vastly outnumber the larger ones because the Devil has succeeded in dividing us into so many factions we feel the need for a church on every corner. I blame the Devil for this because God only divided people into two camps; believers and unbelievers. All subsequent divisions of the brethren have been the work of the Devil. He exploited our tendencies toward self-centeredness to drive wedges between us; a divide and conquer strategy. The result is the scores of denominations we have competing with one another. This division of the body of Christ has diluted our strength and influence. Imagine what we could accomplish if all our resources were pooled and we all pulled together. We could truly be the salt and light of the world.

On the other hand, the large churches that do reap the benefits of economy of scale, don't seem to use those resources to spread the message or improve the lives of others so much as they use them to erect gold plated crystal cathedrals and pay the minister ten times the salary of the average congregant.

There is something disingenuous about a handsomely paid minister wearing a thousand dollar suit in a gold plated sanctuary preaching on tithing as though we were still a theocracy and under Old Testament law. We are neither. Preaching as though we are, to people who know better, is spreading more cynicism than gospel. Street wise people see the church's emphasis on tithing as just a way of separating folks from their money. You'd have to be pretty naïve to attribute to coincidence the fact that tithing is the only one of the 613 commands of the Old Testament that is regularly preached in modern churches. Tithing, like the doctrines talked about in earlier chapters, was singled out by the church for emphasis, consciously or unconsciously, because it is self-serving. Needless to say, the proponents will always conveniently leave out the fact that when tithing was instituted it was to finance the church, all charitable giving, and the affairs of state. Also left out will be the fact that all levels of government today take up to 40% of gross income to finance the state alone. One might think this heavy tax burden on the believer and the lightened load for the church would lead to a reduced emphasis on tithing and more emphasis on charity flowing from the church to the congregation. It hasn't been so.

The church has to be maintained and the minister has to be paid; but ministers making high six figure salaries don't have to take Old Testament edicts out of context in an effort to convince poor people they're going to hell if they don't cut back on their necessities in order to give more to a church that is spending it on opulence. I've seen this happen many times. Ironically, well financed mega churches are the worst offenders. This kind of behavior is not only reprehensible for seeking to take advantage of the less sophisticated among us, it also undermines the churches credibility in the eyes of those sophisticated enough to see through the ruse. As the harvest approaches and tribulation begins, if the church has no credibility, it won't be able to help anyone. We know the Devil is going to prevail against the church for a season, but that doesn't give us the right to abandon the battlefield. We have to come to the aid of the besieged in every way possible.

It is time for Godly ministers to "*think soberly*" about what is going on in the church and call out the charlatans that are teaching self-serving perversions of truth. Failure to do so is a tacit endorsement of their *"doctrines of devils"*. The first amendment to our constitution rightfully precludes the government from any role in limiting those who would twist the gospel to the financial benefit of themselves and/or the church. Therefore, as believers, we must police ourselves. Otherwise, these charlatans will continue to undermine confidence in the church as an institution and further erode its ability to stand as a beacon of hope when the forces of evil launch a full scale war against people of faith. If the church loses its remaining credibility, it will have nothing. The lost sure aren't going to turn to an institution they suspect is just putting out a positive, "feel good" message, in order to separate them from their money. Let's face it; that's what many "ministries" are doing, and many people have seen through it. Once this happens, the church is powerless to reach these people. They're going to have to hear the gospel from someone that doesn't ignite their cynicism.

Until a theocracy is re-established, the church should emphasize offerings instead of tithes, and focus more on how the church can help the congregation instead of how the congregation can help the church. Even more important is the need to call out those who are watering down the hard truths in order to "make merchandise" of the saints. The model can work. I pastored a church for two years; over 100 messages; not one of which was on tithing, or even offerings for that matter. Even so, I think it is safe to say that the average offering, and combined offerings, were both higher when I left than when I arrived.

CHAPTER EIGHT

Aggrandizing

IN CHAPTERS 2 THROUGH 5 we talked about how churches and "the" church draw congregants in with sweet sounding doctrine. In chapters 6 and 7, we talked about why and how they separate those congregants from their money once they are there. In this chapter, I want to talk about issues that relate to both the attracting and the separating.

We have a tendency to put our leaders, spiritual or otherwise, on a pedestal. It has always been so. The self-centeredness that is present in all of us makes our leaders buy into the idea that they are special. Churches and ministers are not immune to this. In fact, church traditions and rituals tend to perpetuate the myth of the minister as a super Christian. It makes it easier for the congregation to justify making personal sacrifices in order to lavishly support the church and, more particularly, the minister. I remember a televangelist once promoting a "name it and claim it prosperity theology" in a message where he pointed out that he had a different exotic car for every day in the week. He proclaimed that it was a measure of his faith and that anyone of comparable faith could likewise have all the desires of their heart. He went on to say God wants to prosper all His people; we just need to reach out in faith and claim all the blessings He has for us. By now you recognize the "name it and claim it prosperity theology" in those lines. Of course he also indicated that one way to demonstrate that faith was to support his ministry. I remember thinking there must have been countless people in his congregation who had made tremendous financial sacrifices for themselves and their families in order to support that kind of gratuitous opulence. Would they have kept their children in shoes with holes in the soles in order to buy him another Bentley if he hadn't already convinced them they'd go to hell if they didn't give 10% of their income? And would he have been able to convince them of that if they hadn't already been taught to view him as some sort of spiritual giant. Apparently this was a guy that would, to quote Christ in Matthew 23:14, "devour widows' houses" to advance his self-interest beyond any rational need.

I'm reminded of all of Matthew Chapter 23 where Christ "reads the riot act" to the so called spiritual giants of His day, the Pharisees. They had used a variety of techniques to put themselves on a pedestal so they could lord over the people. In Matthew 23:5-7, we find Christ saying; *⁵But all their works they do for to be seen of men: they make broad their phylacteries, and enlarge the borders of their garments, ⁶And love the uppermost rooms at feasts, and the chief seats in the synagogues, ⁷And greetings in the markets, and to be called of men, Rabbi, Rabbi.* In Matthew 23:14 He tells them; *¹⁴Woe unto you, scribes and Pharisees, hypocrites! for ye devour widows' houses, and for a pretence make long prayer: therefore ye shall receive the greater damnation.*

The same three ways of perpetuating the myth of the pastor as a super Christian are prevalent today. In the overwhelming majority of churches on any given Sunday, the best dressed person is likely to be the minister. Likewise, the person most likely to offer up the longest and most eloquent prayer is the minister. We could keep going to the most prominent seat in the house, etc., but you get the point.

I'm not suggesting there is anything inherently wrong with anyone, including the pastor, dressing up for church. I would say that if the purpose is to glorify self, it is wrong. If you're wearing a 2 or 3 hundred dollar suit, it's probably out of respect for the pulpit. If you're wearing a 2 thousand dollar suit, it's probably about self-aggrandizement. If you're dressed modestly casual, I don't have to wonder which. I find it very refreshing that a few pastors are beginning to preach in casual attire.

I must say, I'm a little more skeptical about long winded prayers delivered in old King James English replete with "thees" and "thous". From my perspective, any publicly spoken prayer raises questions of motive. God doesn't need spoken words to know our hearts or hear our prayers. The question that begs is that if God doesn't need the spoken words, why are we saying them out loud? If it's for the benefit of bystanders, why don't we just address the bystanders? It seems odd, at best, and deceitful at worst, to be speaking audibly to God when everyone knows He doesn't need the words and bystanders are the real intended audience. I have no problem preaching to crowds and I look forward to my time communing with God; it just doesn't feel genuine when I try to combine the two. I think the Quakers have it right. The best prayer is silent prayer. Prayer should be a lot more about listening than speaking. After all, there is nothing we can teach God, and no limit to what He can teach us. How can we call it prayer when we do all the talking?

Of course there is also the matter of Jesus' teaching and example on the question of prayer. In Matthew 6:5-8 Christ tells us, *⁵And when thou prayest, thou shalt not be as the hypocrites are: for they love to pray standing in the synagogues and in the corners of the streets, that they may be seen of men. Verily I say unto you, They have their reward. ⁶But thou, when thou prayest, enter into thy closet, and when thou hast shut thy door, pray to thy Father which is in secret; and thy Father which seeth in secret shall reward thee openly. ⁷But when ye pray, use not vain repetitions, as the heathen do: for they think that they shall be heard for their much speaking. ⁸Be not ye therefore like unto them: for your Father knoweth what things ye have need of, before ye ask him.* He followed this up by giving us the model prayer that we refer to as The Lord's Prayer. More importantly, He followed it up by giving us a living example of praying in private. Time after time, we see Jesus going off to Himself to pray. Please indulge me pointing out a few of these. *And when he had sent the multitudes away, he went up into a mountain apart to pray…*(Mt 14:23). *Then cometh Jesus with them unto a place called Gethsemane, and saith unto the disciples, Sit ye here, while I go and pray yonder* (Mt 26:36). *And it came to pass in those days, that he went out into a mountain to pray, and continued all night in prayer to God (Lk 6:12).* In Luke 9:28-32 we find that even when He took part of His entourage with Him for a prayer session, He still didn't end up praying before them. *28And it came to pass about an eight days after these sayings, he took Peter and John and James, and went up into a mountain to pray. 29And as he prayed, the fashion of his countenance was altered, and his raiment was white and glistering. 30And, behold, there talked with him two men, which were Moses and Elias: 31Who appeared in glory, and spake of his decease which he should accomplish at Jerusalem. 32But Peter and they that were with him were heavy with sleep: and when they were awake, they saw his glory, and the two men that stood with him.* It would appear the disciples were asleep while He prayed. In Luke 11:1, Christ is apparently praying in the presence of His disciples, but not audibly. It prompts the disciples to ask Him to teach them how to pray and provides another account of Him giving us the model prayer. I'm aware of one instance where Christ prays audibly for the benefit of those standing by. We know that is the reason because He tells us. That instance is in John 11, beginning with verse 41, where Jesus calls Lazarus forth from his tomb. We also know this instance involves a circumstance unique to Christ Himself. *41Then they took away the stone from the place where the dead was laid. And Jesus lifted up his eyes, and said, Father, I thank thee that thou hast heard me. 42And I knew that thou hearest me always: but because of the people which stand by I said it, that they may believe that thou hast sent me. 43And when he thus had spoken, he cried with a loud voice, Lazarus, come forth.* As far as God, Jesus, and Lazarus were concerned, no spoken words were necessary.

I'm not trying to suggest that spoken public prayer is always wrong, or even inappropriate. Although I can't really imagine any of us in similar circumstances, we saw from Jesus' example in the case of

Lazarus, that circumstances really do alter all cases. I am suggesting that spoken public prayer is inconsistent with both the teaching and example set by Christ. Furthermore, I am saying it is a very slippery slope that can easily lead to the kind of self-aggrandizing displays the Pharisees were rebuked for. I must confess that as a pastor and as a visitor in churches, I have often been called on to lead in prayer. To paraphrase the Apostle Paul, when in Rome, I've done as the Romans do; but I have never been comfortable with public prayer. I think the church needs to move away from the practice. Again, I didn't say it is necessarily wrong; but I believe we undermine our credibility in the areas that do impact salvation when we ignore the clear teachings of Christ Himself in matters that don't.

I know there are those saying that Jesus' chastening was directed only at those seeking to call attention to themselves; but is there really any other reason for praying out loud in public? If you don't want to be seen or heard by those around you, the best way to avoid calling attention to yourself is to keep your mouth shut. I would also note that He didn't just chastise the Pharisees and tell us what not to do; He also told us in very clear language what to do; retreat to our prayer closets and pray alone. The rightfully humble and surrendered Christian leaves things in God's hands, realizing God doesn't need our words or our "to do" list. Our prayer time is best spent listening, rather than talking. We don't know what we need, let alone how to express it. When we are right in our spirit, the Spirit makes intercession on our behalf and brings our will in line with God's. Consider Romans 8-26-28; *26Likewise the Spirit also helpeth our infirmities: for we know not what we should pray for as we ought: but the Spirit itself maketh intercession for us with groanings which cannot be uttered. 27And he that searcheth the hearts knoweth what is the mind of the Spirit, because he maketh intercession for the saints according to the will of God. 28And we know that all things work together for good to them that love God, to them who are the called according to his purpose.* We should be self-effacing in our prayer life, not self-aggrandizing.

I would like to note that I don't consider praying with a grieving family, individual, or small group in the hope of bringing them some comfort to be in the same category as the spoken public prayer Christ was discouraging.

Finally, I wish to discuss another area of self-serving aggrandizement that some ministers engage in with the tacit approval of their denominations; the practice of speaking in tongues. Having grown up in a Pentecostal church, I have considerable experience in this area.

First century Palestine was a melting pot of cultures from all over the world. There were scores of languages and countless dialects in use. Simply put, in Christianity's infancy, there were more languages in Palestine than there were Christians. God chose to deal with this by allowing some of His followers to spread the good news to people in their native tongue, or tongues, even if the speaker was not familiar with the language he or she was speaking. We can't know the mind of God of course, but I would assume He knew the church needed a supernatural jumpstart in order to hit the ground running. Overcoming the language barriers by natural means simply would have taken too long. Like a newborn gazelle in Africa, the church had to be up and running almost immediately in order to survive. There was already a lion running to and fro, seeking to devour it.

We find the subject of tongues in several places in scripture. The first is in Acts 2:4-11; *⁴And they were all filled with the Holy Ghost, and began to speak with other tongues, as the Spirit gave them utterance. ⁵And there were dwelling at Jerusalem Jews, devout men, out of every nation under heaven. ⁶Now when this was noised abroad, the multitude came together, and were confounded, because that every man heard them speak in his own language. ⁷And they were all amazed and marvelled, saying one to another, Behold, are not all these which speak Galilaeans? ⁸And how hear we every man in our own tongue, wherein we were born? ⁹Parthians, and Medes, and Elamites, and the dwellers in Mesopotamia, and in Judaea, and Cappadocia, in Pontus, and Asia, ¹⁰Phrygia, and Pamphylia, in Egypt, and in the parts of Libya about Cyrene, and strangers of Rome, Jews and proselytes, ¹¹Cretes and Arabians, we do hear them speak in our tongues the wonderful works of God.* It is abundantly clear from this text that the "tongues" were known languages that were clearly understood by the people in the group who grew up with that language.

The next instance of tongues is found in Acts 10:44-46 *⁴⁴While Peter yet spake these words, the Holy Ghost fell on all them which heard the word. ⁴⁵And they of the circumcision which believed were astonished, as many as came with Peter, because that on the Gentiles also was poured out the gift of the Holy Ghost. ⁴⁶For they heard them speak with tongues, and magnify God...* It seems the witnesses to this event that were converted Jews (*they of the circumcision which believed*) were not as surprised by the miracle of tongues as they were by the fact that such powers were available to the Gentiles. Unfortunately, this passage neither confirms nor refutes the earlier passage establishing that the purpose of tongues was to spread the good news. It does connect tongues with "*the gift of the Holy Ghost*", which we'll talk about later.

The final record of tongues as recorded in the Acts of the Apostles (Acts) 19:4-6 reads as follows: *⁴Then said Paul, John verily baptized with the baptism of repentance, saying unto the people, that they should believe on him which should come after him, that is, on Christ Jesus. ⁵When they heard this, they were baptized in the name of the Lord Jesus. ⁶And when Paul had laid his hands upon them, the Holy Ghost came on them; and they spake with tongues, and prophesied.* This closes out the Biblical record of tongues without calling into question the assertion that the purpose of tongues was to facilitate the early growth and development of the infant church.

Beyond the Biblical record of events involving tongues, there is Biblical teaching on the question of tongues. Except for a curious mention in Mark 16:17-18 (that we'll get to later), all Biblical teaching on the subject of tongues is found in 1ˢᵗ Corinthians 12:10-14:39. In this life, we may never know all of what Paul was dealing with in this passage. The early church record had rightfully established a connection between the Spirit of God being present in a person and speaking in tongues. Based on my reading of this passage, it seems that years beyond the birth of the church, there were those who were trying to trumpet their spirituality by speaking in tongues. Even two thousand years removed from the people under discussion, I can't bring myself to accuse them of faking; it seems so blasphemous. I guess it will suffice to say that the "tongues" Paul talks about in 1st Corinthians differ from those in Acts in that the ones in Corinthians were beyond the understanding of anyone in the audience and therefore did nothing to build the church. Paul refers to these as "*unknown*" tongues. Not knowing their hearts, and without questioning their motives, Paul did not forbid the use of tongues. He brilliantly placed restrictions on their use that, if followed, would prevent people from faking them in order to edify, build up, or call attention to themselves. He did this in one verse; 1st Corinthians 14:28; *28But if there be no interpreter, let him keep silence in the church; and let him speak to himself, and to God.* In other words, if no one understands what you're saying, don't say it. The purpose of tongues was to build the church, not put individuals on a pedestal.

Sadly, even today, we have charismatics trying to build themselves up by faking tongues. Just as in Paul's day, we can't call them on the fact that they speak in tongues because God is certainly capable of bringing this gift of the Spirit back. We can only point out that we will not take them seriously unless there is someone in the audience that can understand what is being said, and if called upon, interpret for the rest of us. As noted earlier, if this is done, it effectively brings tongues to a halt. To my knowledge, there is not one documented case in the last two thousand years of "tongues" being used to cross a language barrier the way it was in the early church. Some miracles of God are for a particular time and place. We see them scattered throughout the Old and New Testaments. Most are one time dispensations. Again, that's not to say they can't be repeated; it merely indicates they are not routine, and certainly not for self-aggrandizement.

Please don't think for a minute that I'm down on charismatics in general. I am not. I grew up in a charismatic church. Even though I ended up being ordained a Baptist minister, I remain very connected to a lot of Pentecostal brothers and sisters in Christ. While charismatics may have more than their share of high profile charlatans in leadership positions, for the most part, their congregations are made up of some of the most sincere and loving Christians you will ever meet. Relatively speaking, they are also diligent students of scripture. I think it is also fair to say they are beginning to see how they may have been misled over the years on many points of doctrine.

The subject of being misled brings me back to Mark 16:17 and 18. Early in my Christian walk, I was being "mentored" by a charismatic minister who suggested that I earnestly seek the gift of tongues. At various points he went so far as to offer coaching on the mechanics of just letting truncated syllables roll off your tongue and the rest would follow. It sounded an awful lot like "fake it 'til you make it" to me. He tried to close the "sale" by quoting Mark 16:17 *"And these signs shall follow them that believe; In my name shall they cast out devils; they shall speak with new tongues"*. Then he resumed coaching on mechanics. At this point, I became rather indignant; righteously so in my opinion. I was personally offended because he apparently assumed I didn't know the verse he quoted was only half a sentence. I considered it an insult to my intelligence, my scholarship, and my spirituality. Even worse, I considered it a sign of disrespect for the Word of God. When I collected my composure, I voiced my angst as diplomatically as possible by asking him to never pitch half a sentence from the Bible to me unless he was willing to live by the whole sentence. The sentence that begins in Mark 16:17 is completed in verse 18. The entire sentence reads: *And these signs shall follow them that believe; In my name shall they cast out devils; they shall speak with new tongues; They shall take up serpents; and if they drink any deadly thing, it shall not hurt them; they shall lay hands on the sick, and they shall recover.* I don't agree with this minister's interpretation of Mark 16:17 any more than I agree with the snake handlers view of Mark 16:18; but I can at least appreciate the fact that the snake handlers have enough respect for the Word not to cherry pick half sentences in order to push their doctrines. Ignorance is just a lack of knowledge, an easily remedied condition we've all found ourselves in at times.

Likewise, we have all made mistakes; almost all of which can be fixed. But intentionally cherry picking the Word of God in order to mislead people is neither ignorance nor error; it is a manifestation of evil.

My understanding is that this passage in Mark was primarily aimed at the apostles. If you look carefully at the list of *signs* that will *follow them that believe* in Mark 16:17-18 you'll notice that most of these things were carried out by the apostles in the early church and are recorded for us in the New Testament. There are no Biblical records of handling serpents in the manner in which it is practiced today; nor is there any record of ingesting poison. But, for obvious reasons, the Bible doesn't contain a record of every event involving every apostle. I would assume there were instances involving an apostle or apostles taking up serpents and ingesting poison. I would not assume it was done ceremonially or in the manner practiced by modern day snake handlers. You may recall the Apostle Paul was bitten by an apparently very venomous snake and felt no effects from it. *³And when Paul had gathered a bundle of sticks, and laid them on the fire, there came a viper out of the heat, and fastened on his hand. ⁴And when the barbarians saw the venomous beast hang on his hand, they said among themselves, No doubt this man is a murderer, whom, though he hath escaped the sea, yet vengeance suffereth not to live. ⁵And he shook off the beast into the fire, and felt no harm. ⁶Howbeit they looked when he should have swollen, or fallen down dead suddenly: but after they had looked a great while, and saw no harm come to him, they changed their minds, and said that he was a god.* (Acts 28:3-6) If you read this passage carefully, you can get the image of Paul bending way over to lay the bundle of sticks on the fire and standing to find the snake hanging from his hand. Apparently, when he lifted himself back up, he also "took up a serpent". I don't know if this is what Mark meant by "take up serpents", but I'm pretty sure he didn't mean believers should tempt God and fate by ceremoniously handling snakes; just as I'm pretty sure he didn't mean they would speak in tongues just to call attention to themselves. There is an Old Testament prohibition pertaining to tempting God in Deuteronomy 6:16. Jesus confirmed it in Matthew 4:7.

Please don't get the impression the gentleman who would have been my "mentor" is indicative of most charismatic believers or the charismatic church as a whole. The opposite would be true. In my nearly 50 years of observation, the Pentecostal church has moved steadily away from these types of charlatans. "Tongues" are rarely heard in a modern Pentecostal church. During this time the Pentecostal church has also shed perhaps hundreds of legalisms as the "Bereans" among them have brought out the truth of the Word. It is one denomination that appears to be moving in the direction of doctrinal truth. Consequently, I expect it will be the group of believers most inclined to receive the ideas in this book with an open mind and search the scriptures to see if they bear scrutiny. Needless to say, I strongly encourage anyone who reads this book to hold it up to the light of God's Word.

We've talked about four different ways people within the church, particularly leaders, engage in self-promotion. Jesus chastised the Pharisees to the point of name calling for three of these; fancy dress, eloquent prayers, and occupying the chief seats at gatherings. I don't need to tell you Christ was not easily provoked to judgment. For the woman caught in adultery, His pronouncement was *Neither do I condemn thee: go, and sin no more.* Yet, for their self-promotion, Jesus declared woe unto the Pharisees and described them as hypocrites, blind guides, serpents, a generation of vipers, and children of hell (Mt 23). The fourth method of self-aggrandizement we talked about, tongues, was not around until after Jesus' death, burial, resurrection, and ascension. If used for self-promotion, it's logical to assume Jesus would have the same opinion of its practitioners.

I understand that the ways in which church leaders call attention to themselves and what motivates them to do so are tedious subjects, because we can't know the minds or hearts of others. But when the church sees that all its methods fit into an overall pattern that is self-serving, it has a duty to think very soberly about the motives behind those methods. If we are not vigilant, dark forces, working at a subconscious level, can steer us toward choices that benefit us in some immediate, superficial, and personal way, while undermining the church and costing us our souls in the long run. The Devil is always trying to make this trade. You may recall he even tried to pull off the trade with Christ when he tempted Him in the wilderness (Mt 4:8-9). Satan's trick is to hold out the carrot while hiding the stick. Our predisposition toward self-seeking makes it nearly impossible for us to see through the deception because our own hearts and minds are set against us. Remember Jeremiah 17:9; *⁹The heart is deceitful above all things, and desperately wicked: who can know it?* We have to ask ourselves if these practices, or doctrines if you will, would be able to stand in light of Jesus' teaching on the subject if self-aggrandizing was not a factor?

Obviously, I believe the church has a lot of work to do in terms of purging itself of the dubious doctrines and self-serving rituals designed to tickle the ears of congregants and elevate church leaders. Regardless of intent, these doctrines and rituals are more effective at paving the way for the Antichrist than helping the lost. It's pretty clear from Revelation that the Antichrist will use warm fuzzy promises, signs and wonders, self-promotion, and ritualized piety to cement his status as supreme leader. A church that has been employing the same techniques will have an awfully hard time convincing people they shouldn't fall for these methods.

CHAPTER NINE

The Road To Hell

I DON'T MEAN TO be flippant about such a serious matter, but I do want to be direct and honest. The world has a date with Armageddon and there will be hell to pay along the way. Not surprisingly, this proverbial road to hell is being paved with good intentions. Secular society and the church are both involved in the paving. They're coming at the destination from different directions but they'll be there at the same time. Society doesn't deteriorate to the point of the government dependence portrayed in Revelation 13 overnight. It has been a long road and paving is still under way. Likewise, the influence of the church didn't deteriorate to the point of it being the non-factor portrayed in Revelation overnight. The churches strength and influence is waning on a pace that parallels the decline of liberty and independence in civil society. By Revelation 13 both will have declined to the point that paving will have reached that figurative hell known as The Great Tribulation Period. At that point, only an act of God will be able to save us from ourselves. Voila; that's why He steps in at Revelation 14! (Mt 24 & Rev 14)

In Revelation 13 we see a one world government that controls all commerce and a puppet "church" allowing that same government to pull all the strings. There does not seem to be any large scale organized resistance to these two facts. As noted, these things didn't happen overnight. It is the result of people being conditioned over time; the boiling frog analogy.

Society is being led to Revelation 13 and the point of accepting complete government dependence by leaders that are gradually getting us to trade little bits of liberty for security. As our country's founding fathers opined, the end result of trading liberty for safety is that you end up with neither. The supposed good intentions our secular leaders are paving the road to hell with are the so called social safety nets and cradle to grave entitlements to help the "less fortunate". Given the pace that taxes have increased as a share of GDP in just the last century, it is only a matter of time until the government controls all commerce and we are all "less fortunate" and totally dependent. Hello Revelation 13.

The church is paving its section of the road to hell by watering down its' doctrines in ways that will make the saints less inclined toward, and less capable of, resistance. Ostensibly, the good intentions behind these changes were to reach more people and help them find more peace and security in their Christian walk. The saints have been fed a steady diet of "itching ears theology" for so long spiritual warriors are already a rare breed. By the time we get to Revelation 13 they will not exist in numbers sufficient for any meaningful resistance.

Chapter Ten

Church's Good Intentions
(PAVEMENT ON THE ROAD TO HELL)

WE'VE ALREADY TALKED ABOUT the various doctrines and their Biblical basis, or lack thereof. As in earlier chapters, we continue to assume that most ministers, lay people, and churches are sincere in their beliefs and their intentions are good. Unfortunately, I believe the church of today is much like the one in Jesus' day; it's made up of "*blind leaders of the blind*" (Mt 15:14).

It's important to note that we don't have to have evil intent in order to be used by the Devil. If we are not fully surrendered to the Lord's will; still motivated by human desires; and blind to a few bedrock truths; we can be led astray and used to pave the way for the Antichrist and his minions. Most of the people doing the Devil's work are doing so unwittingly, with the best of intentions. Let's examine some of those intentions.

You may recall that "easybelieveism" was **intended** to make the plan of salvation easier to understand; lowering the threshold to salvation and making it easier to expand the church; good intentions indeed. The problem is; God didn't leave it to man to set the threshold. He set it Himself, beyond the mere acknowledgment that is the faith of demons. He requires complete surrender. It may not be as easy to explain or understand, and it certainly isn't as attractive to the lost; but there is no victory without surrender. "Christians" that are not fully surrendered to God, will not be empowered by His Spirit and will therefore be powerless in terms of standing against the forces of evil described in Revelation 13. Filling the church with nominal believers that know nothing of surrender is just paving the way for the Antichrist. To paraphrase the Apostle Paul, nominal believers will "fall away" when the ship hits the sand. You're not going to find any martyrs outside the group that is fully surrendered to the Lord's will.

The doctrine of "eternal security" was **intended** to promote peace of mind for those that might be inclined to worry about the status of their salvation. Peace of mind is certainly a good intention. But, I'm going to go out on a limb and say, that if you're inclined to worry about your salvation, then you have reason to be worried about your salvation! If you're worried about it, you obviously failed surrender 101. God made us a promise of salvation if we surrender to His will. If you believe Him, and you have fully surrendered; by definition, you have put salvation and everything else in His hands. If you're still worried about it, you haven't really put it in His hands have you? You need to retake surrender 101. There's a saying in AA to the effect that "if you turn things over without letting them go, you'll be upside down". Unfortunately, that's the state of many Christians today. They continue with doubt, uncertainty, and turmoil because their level of surrender didn't quite reach the level of letting go. They don't know God's unspeakable joy and the peace that passes all understanding because they are not fully surrendered; they didn't completely "let go and let God". They are hanging on to the things they should have turned over, including concerns about their salvation.

A true believer's security comes from their faith; their relationship with God; and their reliance on His promises. If they need the doctrines of man or "doctrines of devils" to feel secure in their salvation, they are in trouble; and so are the rest of us if we're relying on these nominal believers to stand with us against the forces of evil. The doctrines of man and/or doctrines of devils will be subject to change on a whim of the Antichrist and a compliant press will help him bend public opinion to his will. We'd better be relying on something that goes a lot deeper than man made doctrine. Entertaining uncertainty about our condition in the middle of Great Tribulation will be the kiss of death. To quote Winston Churchill; "Nothing is more dangerous in wartime than to live in the temperamental atmosphere of a Gallup Poll, always feeling ones pulse and taking ones temperature."

Church leaders developed the dubious doctrine of "eternal security" because so many within the church were uneasy about the status of their salvation. But why were so many feeling insecure? I'd venture to say it was because they had been welcomed into the church based on another dubious doctrine; "easybelieveism". If you're not fully surrendered, you're going to feel rightfully insecure about your salvation. Oh, what a tangled web we weave. Instead of recognizing the feelings of insecurity as the logical consequence of "easybelieveism" and dealing with the root cause, the church chose to apply another dubious doctrine to mask the ill effects of the first one. People who feel insecure about their salvation should heed Paul's advice from 2nd Corinthians 13:5; *Examine yourselves, whether ye be in the faith…*". Instead of helping them paper over their insecurities, we should have been encouraging them to revisit the concept of surrender. Indulging the insecurities of spiritual pygmies instead of sending them back to the boot camp of surrender is paving the way for the Antichrist.

"Prosperity Theology" was **intended** to give everyone hope for a more blessed and financially secure future. That is certainly a good intention. Of course, it also has the advantage of serving the growth and prosperity objectives of the church and its' leaders. By teaching that prosperity is correlated to faith, and faith is correlated to financial support for the ministry, the church is able to offer a more appealing doctrine in terms of getting people in the door and at the same time provide all its members with a financial incentive to turn their money over to the church and its leaders. In addition, once they've correlated faith and wealth, the opulent buildings and well paid ministers look like badges of honor instead of extravagances in need of an explanation.

I mentioned earlier that the most dangerous lie is the one with an element of truth. Such is the case with "prosperity theology". The power of positive thinking is well documented from both a secular and a religious standpoint. We don't need to reinvent that wheel. The Bible encourages us to be positive in our outlook on life and tells us that such an attitude will lead to greater happiness. I'll gladly stipulate that there is a correlation between faith and happiness.

The problems with "prosperity theology" are that there is no direct correlation between faith and prosperity; no direct correlation between faith and contributions to a ministry; and no direct correlation between the happiness the Bible promises the faithful and wealth. For the most part, "prosperity theology" consists of greedy charlatans and hucksters who appeal to the greed of others in an effort to manipulate them into sending in their money. They set out to convince people that the best way to demonstrate their faith is by giving to the huckster's ministry. They follow this, either directly or indirectly, with a promise that the Lord will re-pay them many times over. While not often overtly stated, they are encouraging people to give in order to gain. They are appealing to their "no one does nought but for gain" sin nature.

I don't know if there are any "ministers" that have intentionally promoted "easybelieveism" and "eternal security" just to assemble a flock of sheep they could fleece utilizing the "prosperity theology" con. I'm not that cynical yet. I do think there are lots of "ministers" that have used "prosperity theology" to take advantage of the large numbers of spiritually immature nominal believers that "easybelieveism" and "eternal security" have brought into the fold. The Antichrist, on the other hand, will have no qualms about intentionally taking full advantage of the stunted believers these "doctrines of devils" have produced. Nominal believers accustomed to constant reassurance of their salvation and being led to expect lavish rewards for no more effort than throwing money at their leaders are going to have an awfully difficult time enduring the harsh realities of tribulation and an even harder time discerning the lies of the Antichrist. After all, he's going to promise many of the same things the charlatans within the church are now promising; salvation, health, wealth, and security. To them the Antichrist is going to seem like the personification of the church; a logical extension of their local minister; a sort of Pope of both Protestants and Catholics. Once again we see the church unwittingly paving the road for him. Remember, Jesus said all but the very elect would be taken in by the deception.

"Escapeism" (the doctrine of a pre-tribulation rapture) was **intended** to offer Christians the hope of getting to heaven without trials, tribulations, or death. Unless you're a bit of a cynic and suspect this doctrine had more to do with corralling sheep to be fleeced than it did with comforting the brethren, you'll have to admit the intentions were good. We'd all like to think we can be transported from hedonism to heaven on a feather bed. Here again, we had a church that wanted to have its' ears tickled and leaders with the financial incentive to provide precisely the itching ears theology required to give them the warm fuzzy they were looking for.

I don't wish to re-argue the case against the pre-tribulation rapture of the church or re-state the arguments for a post-tribulation, pre-wrath harvest. I feel like those cases were adequately made in Chapter 5. I do wish to speak more about how this doctrine is paving the way for the Antichrist.

The successes or failures we find in life's challenges, whether physical, mental, or spiritual, often come down to a question of preparation or conditioning. Success really is 10 percent inspiration and 90 percent perspiration. We wouldn't think of trying to climb Mount Everest or run a marathon without first putting ourselves through rigorous, if not torturous, conditioning. To do otherwise is to invite failure. We wouldn't dare scoop young people up off the street, send them off to war, and order them to storm a fortified enemy position, without first sending them to boot camp where they are mentally prepared to override their instincts and charge into danger rather than flee. How can we expect to create spiritual warriors, capable of enduring incredible hardships of the "Great Tribulation" variety, from people that may not have ever been fully dedicated (easybelieveism) to the cause and have only been coddled with dubious doctrines designed to give them a warm fuzzy feeling? Think about it; once the doctrine of a pre-tribulation rapture was adopted, not so much as the possibility of another scenario is ever mentioned. Except for messages I have preached, I do not recall a single sermon on any other harvest scenario in 50 years of attending protestant churches. Imagine the strain it will put on the faith of nominal believers if this doctrine is proven false and he or she has never been taught about the most plausible scenario, let alone scenarios B or C. Is it any wonder there will be a "falling away" from the faith?

The Devil has been trying to devour the church ever since it was born. First he diluted its strength by breaking it into countless competing factions that we call denominations. Then, he began to further dilute its strength by introducing warm fuzzy doctrines that soften the resolve of the individuals that make up the various factions. This has gone on to the point that the church no longer has the will to engage in the spiritual warfare that reached a fever pitch a few decades ago. But it is much worse than that. The notion of "escapism" has caused so little emphasis to be placed on the timing and nature of the deception the world will face leading up to the Antichrist that most believers not only lack the will to engage the enemy, they aren't even able to discern that there is a battle underway. The Devil has the church just where he wants it; neutered and on the sidelines. "Escapism" had a lot to do with paving this road.

Suppose events get to the point where the church is forced to acknowledge that, prior to the *"harvest of the earth"*, God is using tribulation to separate His "wheats" from the Devil's "tares" just as threshing separates the wheat from the chaff before one is gathered into the barn and the other is burned. Having dogmatically preached a false doctrine for decades, if not centuries, the church will be in no position to rally a spiritual force to resist the great deception of the Antichrist. In fact, the church calling the Antichrist the great deceiver at that point would be a little like the pot calling the kettle black.

In a similar manner, the ritualized narcissism and self-aggrandizement practiced by religious leaders from Jesus' day to the present, will leave the church in no position to take issue with the ways in which the Antichrist will elevate himself to a godlike status.

CHAPTER ELEVEN

Society's Good Intentions

SOCIETY IS NOT STANDING idle while the church diligently paves its section of the road to the figurative hell of Revelation 13. In fact, society is about half done with its paving operation; stockpiles of good intentions are high; and we have every reason to assume the balance of the paving will proceed on schedule.

The end game is outlined in Revelation 13:17. *"And that no man might buy or sell, save he that had the mark, or the name of the beast, or the number of his name."* I won't get bogged down in speculation about the name or the number. The who and what of this verse will be revealed to students of the Word, when we need to know. For now, all we need to know is that the foundation must be laid before it will be possible for one person to acquire that much power. To continue our paving analogy; the top coat of asphalt can't go down until the foundation of base stone is laid. Government control is the foundation or base stone on the road to hell, and control of that government by a single individual will be the finish coat. Authority over our lives has to be ceded to the government before a single individual can take the reins of that government and use it to control us. For now, we just need to be able to see that happening, and recognize it for what it is.

The process of people ceding authority over their lives to government has gone on throughout recorded history. There has been an ebb and flow, peaks and valleys, of human freedom. There are certain things however about the present that make it unique. The framework for a world government is present in the form of the United Nations. Instant, world-wide communication is possible for the first time in history. The widespread use of credit and debit cards, electronic transfers, online banking, social security numbers, tax returns, driver's licenses, global positioning systems, and a host of other technologies make it possible for almost every individual and transaction in the world to be tracked.

So what prompts free people to cede authority over their lives to government and lay the foundation for the road to hell? Good intentions. Government sells them on the notion that there is some problem that is too large for individuals to handle; it can only be solved if resources are collected and pooled. It's an easy sell because people have this innate tendency to buy into the notion that utopia is just around the corner. If we just allow the government to coordinate the pooling of our resources, we can build this great benevolent society; a sort of heaven on earth. As a bonus, we'll get to feel good about our role in the process. Thinking we have taken a step toward helping our fellow man, we get to pat ourselves on the back for being so altruistic.

Two verses of scripture leap to mind; 2nd Thessalonians 2:11 and Malachi 1:10; *"And for this cause God shall send them strong delusion, that they should believe a lie:"* and *"Who is there even among you that would shut the doors for nought?"* Those who would deny mankind's inner depravity and God's pronouncement in Malachi that no one does nought but for gain are indeed victims of a *"strong delusion"*. They grossly overestimate the power of mankind to lift itself out of the mire and they effectively make God out to be a liar by deluding themselves into thinking their own motives are pure. The reality is that all the players have their own self-centered motives. The bureaucrats are simply building their own power base, legacy, or sense of self-worth. The people who advocate for the redistribution of wealth are recipients who expect to be on the receiving end or contributors who want to feel good about helping others and ultimately benefit from the better society they hope to build. Any way you boil it down, everyone's motives are entirely selfish. No one does nought but for gain.

The downward spiral of both religion and society begins with conscious or subconscious denial of the depravity of man combined with delusions about our ability to save ourselves. In religion, the doctrine of "easybelieveism" is born out of the idea, at least subconsciously, that we're not all that bad; a little nip here and a tuck there and we'll be okay. The nip and tuck consist of acknowledging God and making a public profession of faith. The person may now become a fixture in the church while remaining rotten at the core. This nip and tuck formula, contrived by man, leaves out the spiritual awakening / rebirth that God imparts when we completely surrender to His will. In essence, any formula that discounts the vital role of surrender is nothing more than man's shortcut to saving himself; reasoning one's way to salvation. Being in denial over the utter depravity of man prevents the church from seeing the necessity for total repentance and surrender and puts the church on the path to not just paving the way for the Antichrist, but actually becoming one of his unwitting accomplices.

Almost universally, the church has bought into the notion that the government's intentions are good; that collectivism is the way to build a better society; and the church should encourage the government to assume responsibilities once shouldered by the church; such as caring for the less fortunate. Of course the church didn't back off the request for tithes when they encouraged the state to assume this role. The church and state decided it would be okay to just reach deeper into the pockets of those of us who are becoming de facto servants of the state.

It is no wonder that bureaucrats are more likely to be in denial about the depravity of man and delusional about our ability to bring about utopia. For the most part they haven't even been introduced to the concept of the depravity of man. Many earnestly believe that if we will just enact the right combination of plans and policies we can build a sort of utopia, or heaven on earth if you will. The good intentions with which society is paving its section of the road to hell are born out of this mindset.

All the social safety nets such as social security, welfare, unemployment insurance, aid for dependent children, food stamps, disability, etcetera, etcetera, were sold to us as a way to improve society; bring us closer to that utopian vision we were all encouraged to share. So where did it all go wrong? It went wrong in thousands of different ways, all of which have their roots in the depravity of man. Socialism fails because it ignores the God given fact that "no one does nought but for gain". Capitalism succeeds because it takes full advantage of that fact.

While it isn't possible to catalog all the failings of the social safety net, I do want to discuss a few of the more obvious wrong turns.

Social Security was **well intended**. The government was going to take a little out of our paychecks each pay period and invest it on our behalf and in our names. This was supposed to provide a "safety net" so that everyone would have at least a reasonable retirement income. The problem is the government did not invest the money on our behalf and in our name. They spent the money they took from early participants and hid the theft by paying the first wave of retirees out of funds they took from later participants. Now that the number of new participants has declined to the point that their contributions are no longer able to cover the payments early retirees have a right to expect, the government has been forced to admit the earlier contributions were not invested; they were spent. This is identical to the investment scheme for which Bernie Madoff is serving time in prison. I take that back; at least Bernie's contributions were voluntary. Our government, on the other hand, after stealing the money contributed by one generation, compels a later generation to finance payments to the first, so they can pretend they didn't steal the initial contributions. Unlike Mr. Madoff, our elected representatives didn't go to prison because they've made themselves exempt from many of the laws to which they subject us. Instead, most of them were re-elected because they used at least part of the money they stole to buy the votes they needed. This is but a foretaste of what we can expect when people look to the government for provision.

Ultimately, the fraud the government perpetrated on the people with the social security Ponzi scheme and the generational theft it engages in to cover it up isn't the worst problem. The bigger issue is the fact that they have now trained generations to depend on the government for retirement.

Remember, mankind in its fallen condition, is totally depraved. No one does nought but for gain. The government cannot be trusted to spend our money wisely any more than the people can be trusted to elect representatives that place the national interest above self-interest. People will vote based on self-interest, even if it bankrupts the country. And when it does, they will take to rioting in the streets in an effort to persuade other countries to subsidize their feeding at the public trough. The recent austerity riots in Greece are a grim reminder of this. It has been observed by a number of notables throughout history that a democracy cannot exist for long once people realize they can vote themselves money from the treasury. From then on, they elect representatives based on who promises the most benefits, and the democracy collapses in bankruptcy. Does this sound familiar? Many of the European democracies are already there and the United States is accelerating toward the same outcome.

Welfare was **well intended**. It was to provide a minimum standard of living that would keep people from falling into abject poverty. No one wants to see people having to do without the basic necessities of life; food, shelter, and clothing. We're also happy to provide them the tools they need, such as an education, to climb permanently into the middle class. The problem is the axiomatic truth that anything you tax you get less of and anything you subsidize you get more of. A country that taxes productivity and subsidizes sloth will not prosper long. I'm not promoting social Darwinism. I'm not suggesting we should ignore poverty. I am suggesting that when assistance came from the local church instead of the federal government, it was easy to attach strings; place limits; and insure that the industrious weren't being asked to permanently subsidize the lazy. That's where many of us feel we are now. When we see an able bodied family use an EBT card to buy their groceries; while texting on their Blackberry; then use cash they got from swiping a welfare debit card at the ATM to purchase a carton of cigarettes and a case of beer; drive away in a chromed out Cadillac SUV for their home or apartment paid for by the taxpayers under Section 8, we are confident that a line of common sense has been crossed. The unrestrained transfer of money from the productive to the unproductive eventually stifles the incentive of both. Sooner or later, both groups resign themselves to being wards of the state. And we are back to the dependence issue.

I could go on and on about welfare abuses. There are hundreds, if not thousands, of programs; each with constituencies skilled at exploiting them. We have gotten to the point that nearly 50% of the American people pay no federal income tax at all, and nearly 50% of all the households in America receive some sort of taxpayer subsidy from the government. How many of these people do you expect to vote for candidates promising to rein in government spending? But, I don't wish to get bogged down in the details of how the programs are abused or belabor the doctrine of the depravity of man. The present issue is with the dependence these programs foster and how this dependence paves the way for the Antichrist and the events of Revelation 13. Once a significant majority becomes dependent on government, the stage is set. All the Antichrist has to do is rise to the pinnacle of government and he'll have virtually unlimited power over all the people.

Revelation 13:17 makes it clear that government will take over more and more of the economy until people become dependent on the state for their livelihood; "... *that no man might buy or sell, save he that had the mark...*" We are marching in that direction at remarkable speed. In 1903 government spending as a percentage of all the goods and services produced in this country stood at 7%. In 2009 it was 43%. You don't have to be a mathematician or a prophet to know this is headed toward complete government control of the economy, and our lives. To illustrate how much the pace has accelerated in recent years, consider that almost 15% of the total increase in government spending from 1903 to 2009 came in the one year from 2008 to 2009. Of course this says nothing of the fact that government is now proposing to take over, in one fell swoop, an additional 17% of the U.S. economy in the form of health care. When we get to the point where half the people are receiving direct taxpayer subsidies without paying any taxes themselves, and almost 100% of the population is depending on government for their health, and perhaps their very lives, we will have reached the tipping point, and the republic we were bequeathed by our founders will fall off the cliff instead of gradually rolling downhill toward the dictatorship of the Antichrist.

At that point, anyone advocating for genuine repentance; surrender to the one true God; independence from the Antichrist and his web of control; and fidelity to the true church, will be demonized as some kind of heartless nut case the world will seek to purge. This scenario plays out with God's two witnesses portrayed in Revelation 11. They come and preach to the inhabitants of earth until they are overcome by the forces of evil and killed. People rejoice at their passing to such an extent that they leave their bodies on display and exchange gifts among themselves. As Christ warned his followers in John 16:2; *"They shall put you out of the synagogues: yea, the time cometh, that whosoever killeth you will think that he doeth God service."* Once people have been completely *"turned unto fables, they will not endure sound doctrine."* Telling people that the false sense of security they're getting from bowing to the government of the Antichrist is coming at the price of their soul; is not going to be a popular message. I'm reminded once again of the wisdom of our founding fathers in stating that those who would trade liberty for security will end up with neither; and a government big enough to give you everything you want is also big enough to take everything you have.

Chapter Twelve

Collaborative Confusion

To CONTINUE MY ANALOGY of two crews ("church" and state) converging from different directions as they pave with good intentions the road to the figurative hell of Revelation 13, it shouldn't surprise us that some collaboration would take place as the two crews begin to come together. An argument could be made that by not resisting the government takeover of charity, the church collaborated in the creation of a society comprised of dependents and co-dependents. Certainly the incentive was there. The government assuming the role of looking after the downtrodden freed up church funds so the leaders could receive more pay and the buildings could be more opulent. But I'm willing to assume the church acquiesced more than it collaborated in this effort. It's easier to forgive the church for not defending its turf than it is to forgive the church for not protecting the Word.

It is worthwhile to quote John 1:1and 1:14; *"In the beginning was the Word, and the Word was with God, and the Word was God." "And the Word was made flesh, and dwelt among us..."* It is not a trivial matter. If the Word is God, and Christ is the personification of the Word, the Word must be handled with indescribable reverence. I don't mean the ink stains on the paper, they are just that; I mean the concepts and precepts those words lay out for us must be guarded with our lives.

The Word of God has been inspired, recorded, preserved, and passed down to us by the divine providence of God through thousands of years. From the tablets containing the Ten Commandments, to the Torah, to the complete Old Testament, to the Bible we have today, He has made certain that His Word was there to guide every generation. It will not only direct us toward the proper course of action, it will also illuminate the path. *"Thy word is a lamp unto my feet, and a light unto my path."* (Ps 119:105)

Throughout history people have translated the scriptures into many different languages to make them available to more people. After the invention of the printing press in 1450 AD, a large number of translations were printed. I believe the hand of God was involved in this process as well. Between the invention of the press and the explosion of translations, the Bible had never been more accessible. However, the proliferation of translations, some of which may not have been either scholarly or inspired, eventually became problematic.

In 1603 King James commissioned an effort to compile a master English version of the Bible. It was not intended to be a new translation per se. The scores of scholars, bishops, and clergy he assigned to the task were to use the original text and a handful of existing translations, with particular emphasis on the Bishops Bible. Changes were to be made only where changes were warranted by fidelity to the original text. Again, the idea wasn't to throw out all previous translation efforts; the plan was to improve upon those efforts. King James made all the kingdom's resources available, but left the details to those presumed to be led by the Spirit of God and fidelity to truth. It is an effort with no equal in history. Fifty-four scholars were selected and 47 of them dedicated themselves to the task for nearly 8 years; to say nothing of the countless bishops and clergy charged with reviewing their work.

I freely confess that in terms of technical translation accuracy, modern scholars, if they are so inclined, can find things to nit-pick in the King James translation of the Bible. Even so, I remain convinced that it is perfect in the sense that it is the word God intended us to have for the past 400 plus years. You may recall a scene from the book of Acts where the learned theologians of the day were debating what to do about the apostles and their teaching; specifically whether or not to kill them. A very well respected Dr. of the Law named Gamaliel ends the debate by standing up and uttering a timeless truism that I believe is applicable to the work of the scholars that translated the King James Bible; *"...if this counsel or this work be of men, it will come to nought: But if it be of God, ye cannot overthrow it..."* (Acts 5:38-39). His point was that time would tell whether or not the work before them was the work of God or man. By this measure, one cannot escape the conclusion that the hand of God was involved in the translation of the King James Bible. Four hundred years after its completion, it was still the most widely used Bible in the world. All other Bibles in use at the time it was translated, including the ones utilized by the translators, were long ago relegated to the status of relic.

In light of the above, I trust you can understand why I view the modern explosion of Bible translations with considerable skepticism. It's possible that one of the new ones will emerge as the word God wants us to be guided by for the next 400 years, but until it does, I think we'd be well advised to stay with the translation that we can already see the hand of God in. There is no advantage, and considerable risk involved, in hastily shelving one time tested translation in favor of scores of Johnny come lately translations.

I know the Devil is the author of confusion and deception. The door is opened to both by the current proliferation of translations. Traveling from church to church as I do, I'm beginning to see more and more non-KJV versions being used in pulpits. This is true even in what might otherwise be considered "conservative" evangelical churches. It is confusing in terms of trying to follow along with the reading. The potential for deception lies in the fact that it is a virtual certainty that the hand of God was not involved in every modern translation. Consequently, it is also a virtual certainty that the Devil's hand was involved in some of them. Even if that were not the case; the mere existence of so many different translations can be a tool of deception. If this translation doesn't say what you think it should, one of the other hundred or so might. And if a hundred or so other individuals or groups are entitled to come up with their own translation, who's to say you're not entitled to develop your own? Eventually, everyone has their personal favorite and everyone has forgotten the one version that has actually stood the test of time.

The Devil could never take out the Word of God in any direct way. But with so many suspect translations out there, he doesn't have to. Remember the fable about the gentleman who tricked the leprechaun into telling him where his treasure was. It was under a bush in a huge field of very similar shrubs. He tied a ribbon around the bush the treasure was under and made the leprechaun promise he wouldn't remove it while he went for a shovel. When he came back, the leprechaun had kept his promise not to remove the ribbon, but he had tied an identical ribbon on every bush in the field. This seems to be the Devil's strategy. He knows the Word of God is out there and he is powerless to remove it. Instead, he is trying to obscure it by putting out hundreds of similar versions. Another, perhaps simpler, way to explain is that if every version is sacred, no version is sacred. If anybody, and everybody, is entitled to their own translation, and they are all to be given equal weight, there is no sacred Word of God.

Again, the church would be well advised to stick to the Bible that we know God had a hand in, as evidenced by the process of its translation and the 400 year test of time it has withstood. I did not elaborate on the translation process itself as it relates to the King James Version because a full discussion would require a separate book; but please, go online and research the process and the edicts that directed the work. It is a fascinating study that should convince anyone that God's hand was involved, even without the 400 years of history.

This chapter is entitled "COLLABORATIVE CONFUSION" because it isn't just the church that's involved in the proliferation of translations; secular society is also getting in on the act. Indeed, many of today's translations are the work of secularist. Obviously, prayerful consideration was not one of the tools used to arrive at the truth in this kind of translation. Atheists even have one or more translations of their own. But if we haven't drawn any distinctions between the version that has stood the test of time and modern renditions, we have no basis for excluding even the one's translated by atheists. Some lines needed to be drawn, and they should have been drawn a long time ago.

Unfortunately, the church is not into drawing lines these days. A few decades ago, when the church was into drawing lines, they were drawing the wrong lines. The church was developing softer, gentler doctrines and arguing about proper attire and make-up while the government took over education and charity. Putting it another way; the church was "straining gnats while swallowing camels". A couple of generations later, our children have been indoctrinated by a secular, socialized education system and most of us are dependent on government in one way or another. Prayer and Bible reading have been removed from our schools and all vestiges of religion are being purged from the larger society. The proliferation of Bible translations and the equal treatment of same has cheapened them all and opened the door even wider for "more itching ears theology". Our kids have been indoctrinated to think this is enlightenment.

CHAPTER THIRTEEN

Subterfuge Through Subtlety

My GUESS IS THAT some of you are thinking there is a lot of hair splitting going on here. Is there really such a big difference between faith and saving faith? If one hears the gospel, accepts its validity, recites the "sinners prayer", makes a public profession of faith, follows with baptism, and begins to attend church regularly, how can they be lost while the thief on the cross beside Jesus goes to heaven? As noted in earlier chapters, salvation is not an algebraic formula. There is no sequence of words or deeds that will cause God to overlook a haughty spirit and force His way into a hard heart. Remember Psalm 34:18; *"The LORD is nigh unto them that are of a broken heart; and saveth such as be of a contrite spirit."* The Pharisees kept every jot and tittle of the letter of the law. It could be said they followed the formula to a tee. But in the end it isn't about the formula or letter of the law. Their hearts were hard and their spirits were proud. The thief on the other hand, knew nothing of formulas and would not have had time to carry them out if he did. He believed and surrendered to the Lord's will. His calling out to Jesus; *"...Lord, remember me when thou comest into thy kingdom."*(Luke 23:42) was evidence of faith. The fact that he did not seek to avoid the consequences of his actions, but rather rebuked the other thief for asking Jesus to spare them all the cross, shows genuine contrition and acceptance of the Lord's will. Apparently his heart was broken, his spirit was contrite, and he was surrendered to the Lord's will. He had no specific request; he made no demands; he did not seek to be miraculously spared the consequences he had brought upon himself. He didn't need a formula and he didn't have to carry out any procedures or take any actions. In fact he didn't need to say or do a thing. His words are recorded for our instruction; they weren't necessary for his salvation. His acknowledgment had combined with repentance and surrender to produce the broken heart and contrite spirit that must be present before God will convert our head knowledge into the faith that brings salvation.

By placing a counterfeit path (acknowledgment, sinner's prayer, public profession, baptism, church attendance etc.) beside the real path to salvation (faith, repentance, surrender), Satan has done what he has always done; presented *"...a way that seemeth right unto a man, but the end thereof are the ways of death."* (Proverbs 16:25). The difference between God's plan and Satan's plan will always seem subtle to the unsaved. But subtlety is what Satan and spiritual warfare are all about. Genesis 3:1 tells us; *"Now the serpent was more subtle than any beast of the field which the LORD God had made."* I do not expect the Antichrist to publicly deny God or His Word; certainly not at first. I expect him to subtly manipulate the Word of God in a way that elevates him to the status of god, even if he doesn't lay direct claim to that title. I expect him to employ clever, sophisticated, artful, and strategic deceptions that vary only in subtle detail from the truth. This is subterfuge through subtlety. Remember, the Bible tells us all but the very elect will be duped. Again, I remind you that the most dangerous deception is the one that is closest to truth.

The Antichrist is not going to show up on the world stage with horns, a pointed tail, and a pitchfork. He won't be wearing a name tag saying Antichrist. He is infinitely more likely to have an angelic appearance. Think of 2nd Corinthians 11:14; *"And no marvel; for Satan himself is transformed into an angel of light."* He will not be touting his way as the way to eternal damnation; he will be promoting it as the path to enlightenment and utopia; in other words, heaven. I expect he will be promising just about everyone just about everything. It's no different from the false promise of enlightenment he held out for Eve in the garden. *"For God doth know that in the day ye eat thereof, then your eyes shall be opened, and ye shall be as gods, knowing good and evil."* (Gen 3:5). In other words, he'll be preaching "prosperity theology". Just follow my lead, and you'll be healthy, wealthy, and wise; *"ye shall be as gods"*. He even promised Eve a version of everlasting life or "eternal security". In Genesis 3:4 he tells Eve; *"Ye shall not surely die:"*

We know the chief weapon of the Antichrist will be deception. The events portrayed in Revelation make it apparent that the instruments of that deception will be government and the media. Government will be the instrument of the Antichrist simply because it is the mechanism whereby the masses are already controlled, deceived, and manipulated. Even without the Antichrist at the helm, the level of deception and manipulation the government engages in to maintain control over our lives is breathtaking. Because the media is generally comprised of people who believe a benevolent government can lead us to utopia, they generally spin the news in ways that promote more government control. They will succeed in lulling the people into letting the government collect more and more power. By the time they realize the government is not benevolent, and the place we're headed is not utopia, it will be too late. Like the church, their credibility will be shot and the Antichrist will control them also.

The Social Security Ponzi Scheme is an example we talked about in Chapter 11. The promises about who would own it; how the money would be handled; the maximum amount to be withheld; and the guaranteed rate of return, were all lies. The untold truths were even worse than the lies. For example, no one mentioned the fact that whatever wealth you accumulated in Social Security would forever be out of your reach. The government would have complete control over the money and would dole it out to whomever they choose at whatever times and in whatever amounts they would from time to time deem appropriate, without regard to whether or not the recipients had paid into the system. They also failed to mention that based on mortality rates applicable at the time, there was a pretty good chance you'd never see a penny of it come back to you or your posterity. If you can't control it while you're alive, or will it to your children when you die, it was never yours.

If the whole truth had been told, the people may not have approved Social Security. Of course the people wouldn't have approved, even with the lies, if they had just applied a measure of healthy skepticism. There is no historical precedent for a government taking money from its people, managing it well, and returning more than it collected. The very act of collecting and micro-managing the re-distribution ends up being so costly that, even with honorable intentions, a reasonable rate of return is impossible. The people who set it up or agreed to it fit into one of three camps: they were charlatans; they were delusional; or they just didn't think. Those who wanted to grow government just to feather their own nest were the charlatans. Anyone who thought it would be a good investment was delusional. And of course the majority was too busy making a living to give it much thought. Hitler knew what he was talking about when he said; "How fortunate for governments that the people they administer don't think."

Of course Social Security is one of the better government programs. Time and space would not permit us to delve into even a fraction of the 69 different means tested federal programs that provide services to poor and low income families in the United States. Of course the fact that there are 69 different programs with 69 separate, but overlapping, bureaucracies goes back to my point about most of the money being spent on the bureaucrats in charge of the redistribution. Although we have spent over 15 trillion dollars (coincidently about the size of the total national debt) since 1964 on a war they told us would be easily won, poverty is substantially unchanged from where it was when Lyndon B. Johnson declared the national "war on poverty". Yet, our government plans to spend another 10 trillion in just the next 10 years. Isn't the definition of insanity doing the same thing over and over expecting a different result? Is it insanity or the delusion the Bible speaks of? Some of the people behind this expansion of government control over people's lives may have good intentions, but they are just pawns the forces of darkness are using to set the stage for the evil to come.

I'll leave it to others to get bogged down in the thousands of little technocratic idiocies within each of these anti-poverty programs. I prefer to focus on the big picture to see why they fail to alleviate poverty but succeed in preparing the stage for the Antichrist. In the macro they fail because they ignore the fact that, apart from the truly disabled, almost all poverty results from a lack of motivation. Many properly motivated people have risen up out of grinding poverty to become extremely prosperous. Conversely, many very wealthy people, especially those who come into money suddenly, have been known to find themselves destitute in a very short time. My mother used to sum this up by saying that "you could give some people an outhouse and in 6 months they'd turn it into a mansion; other people you could give a mansion and in 6 months they'd turn it into an outhouse." The people in this later group cannot be helped by a handout. Regardless of how much opportunity you put in front of them, some combination of stupidity and sloth will keep them from ever putting it to good use. Indeed, giving them a handout just subsidizes their sloth and further diminishes any incentive they might have had to break out of their self-destructive patterns. Remember, it is axiomatic that anything you subsidize you'll get more of. The old timers would sum this up by saying "some people you just can't help". Undoubtedly Jesus had this group and the truly disabled in mind when He said; *"For ye have the poor with you always,..."* (Mark 14:7) Of course this was not a new revelation. Fifteen hundred years earlier, Moses had stated in Deuteronomy 15:11; *"For the poor shall never cease out of the land:..."* Given this clear language, suggesting that we can eradicate poverty by throwing money at it isn't just foolish; it's blasphemous in that it is tantamount to calling God a liar.

None of this is to suggest that the disabled shouldn't be supported; they should. In fact the rest of Deuteronomy 15:11 goes on to say; *"therefore I command thee, saying, Thou shalt open thine hand wide unto thy brother, to thy poor, and to thy needy, in thy land"* The issue is not whether or not we let people starve; we don't. It isn't even a question of whether or not we're generous; we are. The questions are: who is to be generous; who qualifies for the assistance; and are the recipients accountable to their benefactors. The answers are: The people are directed to be generous. They should carry out this directive as individuals or groups of individuals such as churches, charities, etc. Those who qualify are those who are not able to work. It's pretty clear that charity was not to extend to those who could work, but wouldn't. Second Thessalonians 3:10 tells us; *"For even when we were with you, this we commanded you, that if any would not work, neither should he eat."* Yes; the recipients should be directly accountable to their benefactors. This is the only way to keep freeloaders off the dole. This sounds harsh on the surface, but it ultimately benefits both the slothful and the truly disabled in that it incentivizes the slothful to build a better life for themselves and frees up more resources for those truly in need. We could do so much more for those who are not capable of helping themselves if we didn't allow the freeloaders to drain off most of the resources.

When the government assumed the role of nanny and big brother, the direct link between recipient and benefactor was broken. When family, friends, and churches, were in charge of assisting the needy, they had tremendous incentive to get the people they were helping to the point of being able to stand on their own two feet. Recipients that failed to avail themselves of every opportunity for self-improvement would be called to account. This community network that stressed accountability was replaced with a nameless, faceless, distant bureaucracy made up of individuals that are incentivized to expand the roles of the needy rather than reduce them. How ironic; if they actually reduced the roles of the needy, they could find themselves among them! If truly successful, they'd have no job. On the other hand, if they expand the roles, they might have to expand the office and hire more people. Since they'd have more seniority, that might mean a promotion and more pay.

As programs for the needy are presently administered, the incentives all work in a manner that is the opposite of the programs stated goals; toward expanding, rather than reducing the roles of the needy and the bureaucrats who "serve" them. But the system is worse than broken, it is perverse. It is financially bankrupting the country and morally bankrupting the people it purports to help. Beyond that, like all the other programs, it is adding another layer of dependency the Antichrist will use to bring the population under control to the extent portrayed in Revelation 13.

Don't take my word for the destructive nature of dependency or chalk my comments up to conservative ideals. The liberal icon of the left, the patriarch of all progressives, and the father of "The New Deal" stated in his 1935 State Of The Union speech that, "The lessons of history, confirmed by the evidence immediately before me, show conclusively that continued dependence upon relief induces a spiritual and moral disintegration fundamentally destructive to the national fibre. To dole out relief in this way is to administer a narcotic, a subtle destroyer of the human spirit." Amen! Notice the use of the phrase "subtle destroyer"; a very apt description of the Devil and his minions. Or we could take it back a little further and quote Jefferson; "The democracy will cease to exist when you take away from those who are willing to work and give to those who would not." Again, I don't want to get lost in the tall weeds of the specific failings present in each of the 69 individual programs. I'll continue to focus on the reason they fail in the macro and ultimately enslave the individual and destroy the country.

We all know that when a time limit was placed on welfare benefits by the reform act of 1996, the unmotivated simply sought refuge in other programs. Many of them eventually found their way onto "disability" roles where back pain, arthritis, mental illness (including drug addiction), chronic fatigue or any combination of non-severe ailments could put you in line for "disability" payments that would last the rest of your life. Again, I'm not suggesting we withhold support from the genuinely disabled. We should support them cheerfully. On the other hand, in consideration of this support, they should do all they can to minimize the subsidy they need from society by doing all they can for themselves. Before many of these programs were put in place, most of the disabled worked. Some still do. I know paraplegics that are employed 40 hours per week and ask for no assistance. I also know people that spend 40 hours per week planting fence post, while drawing a disability check from their neighbors. These are not isolated cases; the problem is systemic. It doesn't get fixed because the recipients aren't accountable to their benefactors; the link between the two is broken by a detached bureaucrat that has every incentive to keep people on the dole.

It should be noted that since the number of people "disabled" and the payments to them have gone up, the percentage of the disabled that are working has gone down. Anything you subsidize you get more of. Not surprisingly, the average income of the disabled went down along with the percentage employed. The point is that the more they work the better off they are, both as individuals and as a group. It's a double win for society. Society benefits from whatever they produce while at the same time being spared some of the burden of their support.

All of the above programs pale in comparison to the Affordable Care Act, better known as Obamacare. It took all previous programs more than half a century to get nearly 50% of American households to the point of receiving some sort of taxpayer subsidy. If fully implemented, Obamacare will take over 17% of the U.S. economy and bring nearly all the remaining 50% into some level of dependence on government. Even if it had been struck down by the Supreme Court, it would have returned. Its reincarnation might have been more incremental, but it was never in danger of going away. As programs go, it is still an infant; but we are already finding out that it is predicated on lies even more blatant than the Social Security Ponzi scheme. Our government is taking money from the taxpayers who didn't want socialized medicine and using that money to buy advertising designed to convince us we should want it. They're using our money to propagandize us. You can't get more manipulative than that. Think about it; when they and their accomplices in the media couldn't convince us we needed it with free publicity; they used our money to buy advertising designed to sell us something we told them we didn't want.

Whether by socialized medicine, socialized education, over-regulation, or some combination of the three, the march is steadily toward more government authority and less individual liberty. People are gradually being encircled and imprisoned by walls built from the bricks of false promises. As they fall for more and more of these promises, the people cede more and more authority over their lives to the government. The result is that they become more and more dependent on, and thus captive to, the bureaucracy. False promises may be the bricks that form the walls the government is using to imprison and enslave us, but the foundation upon which all the promises and programs rest is the big lie. Hitler famously said; "Make the lie big, make it simple, keep saying it, and eventually they will believe it." The big lie is that there is a free lunch; there can be gain without sacrifice; we can get back more than we put in. Obviously, it isn't usually stated in a direct way, but the implication is always that things will be free, as in the health care promises; or more than we bargained for, as in the Social Security Ponzi scheme. When discussing government programs, if we just replaced intentionally misleading words with factually correct ones, many of the programs would fall. For example, it is patently false and intentionally misleading to refer to any feature or aspect of a government program as being free. There are no "free" government services; there are only "taxpayer funded" services. If the phrase "taxpayer funded" was substituted for "free" when talking about "free screenings", "free contraceptives", or "free procedures" I suspect the health care plan would be even less popular. The TV commercials currently touting all the "freebies" in Obamacare are shameless. These distortions of fact are coming from sophisticated, educated, wordsmiths. It is not an accidental poor choice of words, it is an intentional distortion designed to mislead. Of course, even with the lies about its cost and the misleading words used to describe its benefits, the people still rejected it. Not to be deterred, the government rammed it down our throats anyway. The bureaucrats were not about to pass up an opportunity to create another layer of dependence for almost 100% of the people.

Socialized medicine isn't going to work any better than socialized education. The U.S. spends more per pupil than almost any other industrialized nation, yet we rank near the bottom in achievement test. The kids aren't broken, the system is. Our kids start out very competitive with their international counterparts but the longer they stay in our public school system, the further behind they fall. Home schoolers and private institutions produce much better results for a fraction of the cost. Imagine the revolution that would take place if every parent was given a voucher for the 10 to 14 thousand per year that we currently spend per pupil and schools had to compete for education dollars. In less than a generation our schools and our students would be second to none. Nothing breeds excellence like the threat of extinction. It's time for our public schools to compete for the right to exist. Innovation, spurred by corporations competing for survival, is responsible for almost all our modern conveniences and our present standard of living. If we exempt education from this competition, we cannot expect it to innovate or excel.

The problems with public education are a lot like the problems with social welfare programs; all the incentives work toward building and protecting the bureaucracy rather than accomplishing the mission. This is a major reason why costs keep going up, even as test scores come down. Much is made of student teacher ratios; but an examination of the student administrator ratio would probably be a lot more revealing in terms of exposing the runaway cost of public education.

Another problem with public education is the fact that, like any other socialized institution, it tends to indoctrinate kids toward a collectivist approach to everything. Since public schools look to the government for funding, they are largely insulated from the manner in which competition forces all who will survive in a free enterprise system to constantly innovate and improve. Since they are insulated from it, they have little or no appreciation for the value of competition, capitalism, or free enterprise. So by the time our kids graduate from high school, they'll be behind the rest of the world in the three "R"s but they'll be thoroughly indoctrinated into looking to the government for funding. And thus another generation of would be dependents is created.

Since "no one does nought but for gain", it is certain that the initial proponents of these various programs had some selfish motives. At the same time, I'm sure some very good intentions were involved; after all, the road to hell is paved with those. Ultimately, intentional or not, the result turned out to be generations of citizens dependent on government and more props being placed on the stage being set for the Antichrist. I'm not suggesting that the people who promote the programs that create the dependence are devils. I am suggesting they are, perhaps unwittingly, doing the Devil's work. They are creating a population that is becoming more and more dependent on a government that will someday be controlled by the Antichrist. They are setting the stage for the evil to come.

CHAPTER FOURTEEN

Winning

I MENTIONED BACK IN Chapter 5, there's a pretty good chance that Armageddon will be the final clash between Abraham's descendants, Ishmael and Isaac. Generally speaking, most scholars agree that the descendants of Ishmael are Arab and Moslem, while the descendants of Isaac are European and Christian. Israelites / Jews / Christians claim the "promised land" by virtue of being descendants of Isaac, the child of promise by Abraham's wife Sarah. Isaac's descendants laid claim to the territorial promise when they conquered the holy land around 1272 BC. Eighteen hundred years passed before Mohammed founded the religion of Islam and asserted a claim to the Promised Land by virtue of being descended from Ishmael, the first born of Abraham by his servant Hagar. Since asserting this claim, countless wars have been fought between the two sides and the land has gone back and forth over the centuries. While the Islamic countries presently find themselves unable to drive out the more technologically advanced western (Judeo-Christian) influences in a conventional war, they nevertheless continue to wage covert operations and carry out terrorist acts intended to ultimately reclaim the "promised land". For the past 1400 years the war has never really stopped. There have been pauses and interludes as one side or the other regroups, but it has never ceased. Some Islamic countries aren't even covert about it; they openly state their intent to drive western influences out of the holy land; to wipe Israel off the map. I wish I could say I believe it will be different one day, but I don't. I would so like to be wrong on this point. But, if history is any indicator, we're just waiting for the Islamic world to regroup.

I'm of the opinion that the wars, famines, pestilences, etc. that are the run up to the "Great Tribulation" will be driven by economic collapse and major clashes between the two religions that some are calling a clash of civilizations. Out of the havoc and despair this causes, a false savior will arise claiming to be able to restore prosperity, peace, and tranquility. He will use signs and wonders to convince many that he is indeed "the" savior. Of course this will be the Antichrist. People will unify behind him and grant him unprecedented power only to realize too late that the previous tribulation was a walk in the park compared to what they are in store for. After persecuting the saints to the ends of the earth and martyring them by the millions, he will lead the rest of the world to the slaughter we know as Armageddon. I believe this final battle will take place after the *"harvest of the earth"* or rapture if you prefer. I have every reason to believe that chapters 14 through 16 of Revelation are sequential.

Perhaps a little recap is in order. The "harvest" of the saints takes place in Chapter 14 of Revelation. The wrath of God is prepared in Chapter 15, and poured out on the earth in 16. The wrath of God follows the "harvest". God will not pour His wrath on His own people. The calamities recorded for us in the first thirteen chapters of Revelation are all either man-made disasters or natural disasters made worse by self-serving responses. God steps in just when it appears mankind is about to erase himself from the face of the earth. Remember, Jesus told us in Matthew 24:22; *And except those days should be shortened, there should no flesh be saved: but for the elect's sake those days shall be shortened"*. True to His Word, Jesus steps in and gathers His own before the wrath of God is poured out on the remaining inhabitants of earth. The wrath of God that is poured out in Chapter 16 of Revelation makes the tribulation period before the "harvest" look like a day at the beach. Finally, what's left of mankind, the most callous of the hard core, will be drawn into the final conflict known as Armageddon.

With the church failing in its commission, with society becoming more secularized by the day, with government creating dependents by taking over our lives and consuming our liberty, with economic collapse on the horizon, with terrorism on the rise, and knowing about the world's date with Armageddon, it would be easy to get discouraged. But we should not. The world is going to hell in a hand basket and all we can hope to do is perhaps delay the inevitable. However, we can still win on the two fronts where it really matters. We can avoid being among the duped when the Antichrist comes to power, and we can know that when the period of tribulation that separates the wheat from the chaff is over, we'll be among the wheat. It's a pretty good deal when you think about it; the same deal God has always offered. We can't rewrite the script to change the overall story line, but we can pick the role we wish to play. If we stand on His side throughout, even if we're among the martyrs during the tribulation, we'll be among the winners in the end.